Bridal Shower Themes

Casual to Elegant

Pat Nekola

ISBN Number: 978-0-9796523-5-6

Library of Congress Number: 2011923459

Front and back cover illustration and design by Carol Calabro
Photography by Steve Nekola
Computer Consulting by Debbie Kabitze
Interior color illustration by Carol Calabro, Cathy DeWitt, and Jim Petruzzello
Line art and book layout by Carol Calabro

Published by:
Applewood Ink
A division of: Catering by Design Books

Printed in the United States by
Quad Graphics
Menomonee Falls, Wisconsin

Dedication

I would like to dedicate this book to my husband Steve for his support and all the librarians throughout the United States, my Waukesha Family YMCA, my birthday club for their encouragement and interest in the making of this book, *Bridal Shower Themes, Casual to Elegant.* Their support has helped me to stay focused to create a beautiful book.

About the Cover

Carol Calabro worked to find just the right parasol, flowers, and heart rain drops to create a beautiful cover. She not only used a rose which signifies love and elegance but also tulips. The tulip represents elegance and grace while the fuchsia flower falls down with grace and is noted as the casual flower. She recalls the story of a gallant knight who delivered a tulip to the princess's door step every week. The pathway and stone walk way represent the path ahead of the couple as they make a serious commitment to each other upon being engaged. The cover is filled with brightness and gives the reader a sense of wanting to celebrate by giving the happy couple a bridal shower.

Acknowledgements

I would like to thank my extended family and all my personal and business friends, neighbors, and customers that have spurred me onward and used my professional catering services for various parties including bridal showers.

I would also like to thank Kathy Molnar, Sue Schmitzer and Leo Hickok for editing the book. I also want to thank Susan Horn for helping me with *A Couples' Bridal Shower-Watermelon Theme* and Joanie Hoppe for having the shower at her lake property and for formatting the hearts in the bridal shower book. I want to acknowledge Glen Victorey for several of his creative ideas and lending me his equipment and decorations for several of the shower parties. I would like to thank Uncle Carl for hosting the Grandpa Ray's party at his bachelor's pad. I want to thank John Guay for his participation and making this a great party. I especially want to thank Carol Calabro for all her countless hours and effort to make this book so special. I want to recognize Betty Vogt for helping me on computer challenges, and input on the Rachel shower. I would also like to thank Graphic Xpress for their efforts in helping complete the graphic arts.

Disclosure

I do not proclaim to be an expert when giving bridal shower parties. However, I ran a catering business for 18 years. I did many bridal shower themes. I created just the right theme for each bridal shower and received many compliments on my bridal shower ideas.

I have also authored *Picnics, Catering on the Move* with many creative party ideas for many family and business events.

I have a flair for decorating and also designing recipes to make a party special. Both of my authored books titled *Picnics, Catering on the Move* and *Bridal Shower Themes, Casual to Elegant* are designed to eliminate guessing how much to cook when serving various sized groups.

My goal is to enrich the lives of families by helping them plan parties that are memorable and worthy of a celebration.

Pat Nekola

Introduction

Bridal Showers and Wedding Traditions

The story goes that in the late 1800's family and friends bought or made small gifts and gave them in a parasol. The parasol was opened over the bride's head.

No one is sure of the date or time but a young Dutch miller fell madly in love with a beautiful Dutch girl in the middle ages either in the 1500 or 1600 hundreds. He was very poor. Her father was upset that the Dutch miller had no dowry. Her father told the Dutch miller, "no dowry, no marriage." It did not stop the Dutch girl from running into the arms of the Dutch miller. She insisted on marrying the love of her life. So, the village folks and friends thought that they would help them by setting up a home with many gifts. Impressed by the generosity of the villagers, her father finally accepted that the household gifts and contributions were enough to take care of his daughter. From that day forward it became a custom for friends and family to give the bride-to-be a shower. In modern times showers have replaced the dowry method. Another story from the middle ages is about a knight and a princess. He loved her and grew tulips. He would deliver a tulip to her door step every week. Unfortunately for the knight, the princess was required to marry a man of her father's choice.

There are many customs for various bridal showers and weddings which come from their ancestors in many countries. As far as bridal showers go, the earliest stories say that bridal showers originated in Brussels, Belgium around 1860. In the United States, bridal showers started in urban areas in the 1890's mainly among the upper middle class. However, by the 1930's bridal showers had spread to rural America. Bridal showers are very popular in the United States. In the 1920's, an etiquette guide came out suggesting showers should be purely spontaneous and informal with guests arriving unannounced at the bride-to-be's home. Another planning guide from the 1950's suggests more complex theme showers and games.

Showers have not developed the same formal etiquette as weddings. Keep in mind that a shower is a gift-giving occasion. Everyone that attends a shower is expected to provide a gift. People who decline the invitation for any reason are not expected to send a gift nor participate in the party. If I am invited to a shower and cannot attend, I will send a gift and also call the bride-to-be and wish her well on her upcoming marriage. Use your discretion.

The hostess may send out invitations by mail, telephone or email. Some invitations say regrets only while others will ask for a reply (R.S.V.P) by a certain date.

When I ran my catering business, I was surprised how many people did not reply and thus put the hostess on a spot for giving a final count. I can't stress enough how important it is to respond on the requested date. It is only common courtesy to the hostess.

Wedding Traditions

I found it very interesting to learn about some of the wedding traditions. For instance, a couple in China may get married on the half hour. For example, they may marry at 12:30 p.m. when the clock is on the up-swing. It is believed that the couple will have ascending fortune.

In Bermuda a tree is planted after the ceremony. The tree symbolizes the growth of the love of the couple. In England it is considered good luck if the chimney sweep kisses the bride on the way to the wedding. Sweeps are associated with hearth and home which contributes to domestic bliss. Filipinos wind strands of coins, diamonds and flowers in figure eights around the necks of the bride and groom to show there is a conjugal bond. You might think that a white cake is a sign of the bride's purity. However, in the middle ages the intense whiteness of the cake showed that the cake was very expensive.

My Story

Showers create valuable memories not only for the bride-to-be but also for friends and family. I still remember my surprise shower given by my high school students. Three of my students actually drove to my fiancé's office (now husband) and approached him to drive me to the shower location. They made sure that he understood that the party was a surprise shower.

He treated me to dinner at a very fancy restaurant and then proceeded to tell me that he wanted to stop over at a friend's home. He thought I just might like to meet him. We arrived at the shower location and all the students came out to greet me and yelled "Surprise". Indeed, I was surprised. They had several rolls of white crepe paper and wrapped the crepe paper around my body to create a beautiful wedding gown. They also made a crepe paper veil and took several photos of me in that hand crafted gown. They kidded me and said, "Now you don't have to make a wedding gown. You have the perfect gown to walk down the aisle." I thanked them for the new look.

One of the student's mom was generous and made the food and punch for the party. It was simple and tasty. We sang songs and they told stories about my class. I opened my gifts and enjoyed the evening.

Our co-workers gave us a beautiful sit-down dinner party as a send off one week before our wedding. It gave us a chance to visit and get acquainted with every co-worker's spouse. We enjoyed the evening and all the guests. To our surprise they gave us many beautiful gifts. I still use and cherish these gifts.

I met my husband while working at the same school. My friend and coworker said, "You need to find a man and settle down. The clock is ticking and you are not getting any younger, Pat." She nagged me until I consented. He asked me out and I declined twice before I finally dated Steve.

I called my mother and father and told them that I had met my Mr. Right. My Father said, "Sure you have. Get some rest and you will be fine."

Since age eight, my dream was to have a December wedding. He proposed in August and we were married in December of 1971.

On the evening of the marriage proposal, he talked a lot at dinner. Usually Steve is very quiet. After dinner we drove to our favorite park to walk off our dinner. I still laugh because it seemed like we walked forever around that odd shaped lagoon several times. Finally, he got up enough nerve to ask me to marry him. I accepted. My love for my husband has grown by leaps and bounds and I would marry him again. He continues to buy me flowers many times during the year for no reason and remembers me on special occasions.

How I Became Interested in Catering Parties and Showers

The first seven years of our marriage I did a lot of entertaining because cooking is one of my passions. I also enjoyed making beautiful table settings and centerpieces. I became very interested in catering and worked my summers at our local catering company and also taught food service and general home economics during the school year. I took classes at the local technical school (WCTC) and received training. With my training I taught night classes at the same technical school.

My husband and I decided to open a catering business. We called our business Pat's Party Foods. As I gained recognition for my work and applied my business skills, I designed a course called *"How to Start Your Own Business"*.

As our business grew I received many inquiries on bridal showers and weddings. Many people did not know how to organize a shower and hired our catering service. Throughout the years my experiences have helped me to create the bridal shower book with casual to elegant recipes, love stories, games and decorations for several bridal shower themes. The layout of this book is a step by step guide with easy-to-follow directions and many creative ideas to impress the guests and also to honor the bride-to-be.

Examples of Bridal Showers

The older generation often gave kitchen showers. Other showers may have a clock theme. Each guest received an invitation with the time. The guest is asked to purchase a gift pertinent to the time on the invitation. For example, if the person gets an invitation with 3 o'clock, she could buy a tee time gift for the couple to play golf or movie tickets. A little saying is then written to the couple along with the gift. A lingerie party might be appropriate if the bride-to-be expresses that this theme party is right for her. When giving a couple's party, the shower theme could be sports if they play sports. Couples' showers are becoming more popular. Consider both the bride and groom to-be so that both can attend the party. A drop-by party is an open house party and does not have games. The guest drops by to give their praises of good wishes to the bride-to-be and also visits with her while she opens your gift. Each guest is invited to partake of the buffet filled with finger foods. The guest will leave after partaking of the buffet and thanking the hostess for the invitation to the party and the lovely dessert or appetizer buffet. I have attended a shower at a home where we were required to bring an unwrapped gift. The shower took place at my friend's home via satellite. The happy couple was stationed in Iraq. They watched as her sister showed off the gifts. The guests also talked to the couple. This was a very different shower and gave me a warm and fuzzy feeling. I also attended a shower with 100 guests at a golf course. They served many appetizers and several varieties of desserts. We played several games and quietly talked among our friends. I found that shower to be very long. It took almost two hours to open 100 gifts. It was a very long Sunday afternoon for most of us. I personally prefer attending a shower with fewer guests. It is more personable.

Making Plans for the Perfect Bridal Shower

Each generation may have a different idea on how to select a type of shower. At any rate, select your theme and begin to plan the shower at least 4-6 weeks in advance of the actual shower date. The shower should be at least one month in advance of the wedding. Sometimes it is impossible to have a shower a month ahead of time due to our modern day mobile society. When family is scattered throughout the United States and even foreign countries, a shower may be planned only a week in advance of the wedding to ensure that family members and closest friends can attend both the shower and the wedding. Remember to invite family and close friends to both the shower and the wedding to avoid hard feelings.

For starters, consider the number of showers given for the bride-to-be. Consider the family, friends and the time of the bride-to-be. Also think about the local customs and the couples' taste. Consult the bride-to-be and ask for her input. Select a theme and choose her favorite colors. I catered a shower in April. The bride-to-be's favorite colors were green and orange. I could not quite see those colors as bridal shower colors. However, as I worked out the details, I found that the colors were very eye catching. I learned that it paid to be different for the shower was bright and beautiful. In America, people live to eat and often rate the party with the quantity and quality of food. Hopefully, your focus as a guest will be on the bride-to-be as a participant and not entirely on the food, even though food may be very important to you.

As part of your planning, determine the size of your guest list depending on the size of the space used for the shower. Send out invitations 3-4 weeks before the shower with an R.S.V.P. written on the invitation. The hostess can also use E-vite via email for a causal party. Invitations can be made on the computer and can be very classy. Be sure that you include the date, time, type of shower, location, the name of the bride-to-be (first and last name) and your phone number. If it is a surprise shower make sure that it is very clear on the invitation. Think through your plans and decide what kind of food should be served and what best fits the bridal shower theme. It could be a buffet, sit down dinner, a casual barbecue at a lake, or a simple dessert gathering. Cost may be a big factor of what type of shower given to the bride-to-be. Consider the time of the day when planning the food. If a person holds a shower from 2-5, she can easily serve finger appetizers. The majority of showers are given in the day time and very often on weekends. Sundays are good days, especially if the men are watching sports. Plan a menu to accommodate the guests with a special diet such as a diabetic or vegetarian. The people helping with the shower might know about guests with special diets; hopefully they can alert the hostess. The hostess should not make a big deal about any special diets. She can incorporate foods that all the guests can eat including any special foods. The hostess can decide if she would like to serve the food upon the arrival of the guests or after the gift opening. I like to serve punch and appetizers when the guests arrive. In this bridal shower book, I have expressed that you can make food ahead of time and freeze it until a day before the party. Of course, freezer space must be available and family members must be alerted that the food is reserved for the shower.

Decorations

Sky is the limit when selecting decorations. I find that for elegant parties listed in my bridal shower book, the decorations add greatly to the eye appeal and enhancement of the food service. The right decorations immediately catch the attention of the guests and often become a huge conversation with many sincere compliments and praises for the hostess. Some use balloons or fresh flowers. I decorated a fall shower with a leaf theme and pumpkin dishes for the *Fallen in Love Bridal Shower Theme* in chapter 8. In chapter 9 Aunt Marta decorated *A Berry Beary Christmas Bridal Shower Theme* with a bear theme and used the bear brownies to make a wish to the bride and groom during desssert. In addition she used the color game which created alot of fun and conversation. See page 219.

Pointers for the Hostess

1. Clean your home and take care of every detail and preparation in advance.
2. Always write out your menu and have a check list so that all the foods are served at the party and not forgotten.
3. Cook with recipes that are familiar to avoid any hassles or disappointments on the day of the party.
4. Make sure that there is plenty of food to be able to serve seconds.
5. Set up the buffet equipment and seating arrangement one day ahead of time.
6. Wash and press tablecloths a couple days before the party.
7. Freeze ice cubes a week ahead if freezer space is ample or assign a close family member to pick up the ice last minute. Husbands are good for that errand. It also gets them out of the house and away from under your feet.
8. Make sure that there is plenty of toilet paper, tissues, hand soap, and hand towels for the guests. (When someone uses the bathroom, they notice the decorations and the cleanliness of the room due to their seating arrangement).
9. When designing flower vases, use the appropriate size vases which lend to space for friendly conversation. It isn't fun to talk to guests at your table when a centerpiece is too tall; they can't see each guest's face.
10. Provide a trash bin for the wrapping paper from the gifts.
11. Assign someone in the bridal party to write down the gifts and the person's name giving the gift.
12. Get plenty of help so that you are rested and ready for the party. For a successful party, the hostess needs to be relaxed, calm and gracious.

Gifts for the Bride-To-Be

1. Remember that the bridal shower is in honor of the bride-to-be.
2. People tend to buy gifts they like for themselves. Always consider what the bride-to-be might like and the usefulness in her future home. A bridal registry is most helpful when selecting a gift.
3. If you are very close to the bride-to-be, a handmade gift is often very appropriate. For example, I made a memory book for the shower. The bride-to-be was very pleased.
4. If you cannot make the shower, a gift can be sent ahead of time to the hostess home.
5. Devote a special space for the gift opening with a comfortable seating arrangement and also a good view for guests to see.
6. Pass the gifts and cards around and acknowledge each person's gift.
7. The bride-to-be should always write a thank you note for the shower gifts. Be sure to thank the hostess for a job well done and all her hard work. Somehow a phone call or an email just doesn't seem the most appropriate way to say thank you, but in today's busy world it is acceptable. I prefer to write a thank you note. To me, it shows that you took the time to write a written note and that you really appreciate the guests attending your shower.
8. A thank you note for the gift should be sent within 30 days after the shower.

Guest Etiquette

1. Do not arrive at the shower early for it may interrupt the hostess's last minute preparations.
2. Park near the place of the shower and walk. Do not block the driveway.
3. Be a good listener and also a courteous conversationalist.
4. Be polite and considerate of all the guests.
5. Say your goodbyes inside the hostess's home not yelling from your car.
6. Be sure to thank the hostess for a job well done.

Conclusion

Let's get started organizing a professional bridal shower by implementing tips and ideas from the *Bridal Shower Themes, Casual to Elegant* book. You will look like a professional caterer at the art of creating a memorable bridal shower. This book takes out all the guess work and gives you increments of recipes, shopping lists, charts, games, buffet layouts and more.

Outline of the Names of the Bridal Shower Themes and the Appropriate Season for Each Shower

Part I
Casual Bridal Shower Theme Parties

Part II
Elegant and Casual Bridal Shower Theme Parties

Contents

Topics under Introduction

Chapter 1
An April Shower Bridal Theme

Chapter 2
A Couples' Bridal Shower-Watermelon Theme

Chapter 3
An Open House Engagement and Bridal Shower Theme

Chapter 4
A Drop-by Bridal Shower

Chapter 5
Rachel's Bridal Shower

Bridal Shower Theme Parties Section Part II
Chapter 6
Grandma Kay's Garden Bridal Shower

Part II of Chapter 6
Grandpa Ray's Bachelor Party

Chapter 7
Paris is for Lovers Bridal Shower Theme

Chapter 8
Fallen in Love Bridal Shower Theme

Chapter 9
A Berry Beary Christmas Bridal Shower Theme

Part II of Chapter 9
A Casual Berry Beary Christmas Bridal Shower Theme

Chapter 10
The Engagement Announcement Social by Mrs. T

Part II of Chapter 10
Mrs. T's Bridge Club Party

General Information

Learn how to purchase ingredients in quantity, how to portion recipes, and how to cook with special cooking techniques. Apply the step-by-step line drawings, explanation of buffet and guest table layouts with pictures to make any hostess look like a professional caterer. Using the many tips on how to garnish foods is the key to making the party look attractive, for every guest eats with his/her eyes. When I catered, my slogan was always plenty of tasty food attractively presented.

Design of the Book

The *Bridal Shower Themes, Casual to Elegant* book is designed to help families and friends cater their own bridal shower with style. All the information in this book pertains to organizing and presenting a shower for that special bride-to-be and to help the hostess give a memorable shower.

Understanding the Layout of the Book

The entire book is laid out in chapters with a particular bridal shower theme. Each chapter is easy to read with simple directions to put the party together. The tips explain such things as quantities, products, what to buy or explanations of a recipe for clarity. The charts explain quantities for the hostess preparing for the number of guests attending the bridal shower. Whether cooking for a small or a large group, the *Bridal Shower Theme, Casual to Elegant* book is a great guide when celebrating a bridal shower worthy of a celebration. Here is your opportunity to be the perfect hostess when presenting a memorable shower with a flair. Have fun!

Part I

Casual

—

Bridal Shower Theme Parties

Flying Flamingo Pineapple Cheese Tree

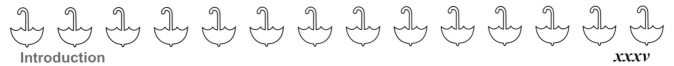

PART I
TITLE OF SHOWERS

CHAPTER 1
An April Shower Bridal Theme

CHAPTER 2
A Couples' Bridal Shower-Watermelon Theme

CHAPTER 3
An Open House Engagement and Bridal Shower Theme

CHAPTER 4
A Drop-by Bridal Shower

CHAPTER 5
Rachel's Bridal Shower

The *Bridal Shower Theme* book is divided into two parts (Part I and Part II). The showers are designed with savory recipes with several written in quantities from 6-50 servings. The tested recipes include appetizers, soups, salads, hot vegetables, main courses, brunch menus and desserts designed for a bridal shower celebration.

Chapter 1
An April Shower Bridal Theme

An April Shower Bridal Theme Buffet Table

Brunch Menu

Appetizers
Finger Cucumber Sandwiches
Stuffed Mushrooms

Main Course
Broccoli Quiche
Ripe Olive Quiche
Chicken Crepes
Fresh Strawberries and Cantaloupe Platter
Ham, Cheese and Grape Platter
Assorted Cocktail Buns
Butter, Mustard and Mayonnaise
Corn Bread Hearts
Orange Coffee Cake

Desserts
Bridal Shower Cake
Chocolate Chip Cherry Flan Torte

Beverages
Orange Sherbet Punch
Orange Juice and Ice
Coffee, Tea, Milk

An April Shower Bridal Theme

Usually the bride-to-be will tell how she met her future husband. I never really got the particulars of how their romance developed. I think that Paula and Erich met at a party. It took them several years to decide to marry. I did the shower and wanted it to be very nice, since I was a friend to the family and watched Erich grow up.

His mom and I selected a brunch menu that we thought would be filling and very attractive. We held the shower in my home. I enjoyed decorating and preparing for the shower. I didn't know many of the invited guests or Paula's family, but I felt very much at ease entertaining them. The guest of honor was very gracious and appreciative for the gift of the shower. People were wonderful and mingled well as a group while wishing Paula much luck. The brunch was laid out on the dining room buffet table using the bride's favorite colors—green and orange. The guests served themselves. All the food was served on china with two guest tables set up for seating. Tables were covered with a tablecloth with a green background and multi-colored umbrellas, a cloth napkin in a napkin ring adorned with an umbrella designed from green cardboard depicting an April shower theme and a game in a bag. More details of this shower will unfold as we begin with the brunch menu served at this April Showers Bridal Shower Theme.

Guest Table Setup

A 1 pound 8 ounce loaf of bread yields 14 slices. One slice of bread yields two finger sandwiches. Cut off crusts for finger sandwiches. You can use the crusts to make dressing or bread pudding.

One large cucumber yields approximately 30 slices.

Butler pass means that a hostess or helper takes a tray of appetizers around the room with napkins at hand and offers the guest an appetizer. The person passing the appetizer hands them a napkin and asks the guests to select an appetizer.

☂ Appetizer Menu

Cucumber Finger Sandwiches
Yield: 40 finger sandwiches

2-8 ounce packages (each)
  cream cheese, softened
1 teaspoon Worcestershire sauce
1 teaspoon onion powder
1 to 1½ loaves (1 pound 8 ounce
  wheat bread)
2 cucumbers
dill weed
2 doilies
2-12 inch trays

Cucumber Finger Sandwiches

Add Worcestershire sauce and onion powder to the cream cheese. Beat until smooth and creamy. Set aside. Using a shot glass or a small round cookie cutter, cut out the bread rounds. Spread each bread round with cream cheese mixture. Wash and dry each cucumber. Run a fork from top to bottom and all the way around the cucumber to make a decorative edge. Slice two cucumbers into circles with peelings. Lay out each cucumber slice out on a paper towel and squeeze out extra moisture. Place one cucumber slice on each bread round. Sprinkle with dill weed. Arrange cucumber sandwiches on lined doily trays and butler pass to your guests. (See cucumber finger sandwiches above).

Tip

There are 20-24 medium to large button mushrooms to a one pound package. A 13x9 pan will hold 28 large mushrooms, 4 across and 7 down.

I like to use the fancy packed white crab meat.

Crab-Stuffed Mushrooms
Yield: 36-40 mushrooms

2-1 pound packages
  large mushrooms
6 tablespoons butter
4 green onions, chopped
2-6 ounce cans crabmeat,
  drained well
2 cups Italian bread crumbs
2 teaspoons minced garlic
3 tablespoons orange bell pepper,
  finely diced
1 teaspoon Worcestershire sauce
½ teaspoon salt
¼ cup Parmesan cheese
1 cup mozzarella cheese, divided
No-stick baking spray
1 doily
1-12 inch tray

Wash and trim the end of stems from mushrooms. Remove stem from each mushroom. Chop stems and set aside. Spray 2-9x13 pans with no-stick baking spray. Place mushrooms in rows with opening of the cap of the mushroom face up. Melt butter in skillet; add the chopped stems, minced green onions and red bell pepper. Cook until vegetables are barely tender. Add the vegetables to the bread crumbs, crabmeat, Worcestershire sauce, salt and Parmesan cheese. Fill each mushroom cap with stuffing and sprinkle with mozzarella cheese. Bake at 350F for 15 to 20 minutes. Place baked mushrooms on the doily lined tray and butler pass.

Tip

A quiche can be cut into 6 large pie shaped pieces or 8 smaller pieces. Most women will prefer to have the quiche in smaller pieces especially if there is a large variety of food served at the party.

The filling for this recipe can be doubled or tripled and still be tasty. When doubling or tripling the recipe, divide the filling between or among the ready-made pie crusts.

 Brunch Menu (refer to pages 84 for illustration of brunch items)

Broccoli Quiche
Yield: 1-9 inch quiche (8 servings)

1-9 inch frozen deep-dish pie shell
1-8 ounce package cream cheese,
  softened
4 eggs
1 tablespoon red onion, diced
½ cup mushrooms, diced
2 tablespoons red bell pepper, diced
2 tablespoons celery, diced
¾ cup broccoli flowerets, chopped
½ teaspoon white pepper
1½ cups grated Parmesan cheese
1 cup shredded mozzarella cheese

Preheat oven to 375F. Beat the cream cheese until smooth. Whisk the eggs. Add the eggs to the cream cheese and beat. Add the red onion, mushrooms, red bell pepper, celery, broccoli, white pepper and grated Parmesan cheese. Pour the quiche mixture into the unbaked pie shell. Sprinkle with mozzarella cheese. Bake for 45-60 minutes, or until the filling is firm.

Ripe Olive Quiche
Yield: 15 servings

1¾ sheets puff pastry
2-8 ounce packages (each)
  cream cheese, softened
5 eggs
1 cup Parmesan cheese
3 cups sliced black olives
1¼ cups mozzarella cheese

Cover the bottom of a 9x13 inch pan with the pastry sheets to form the crust. Beat cream cheese and eggs together and pour over the pastry. Sprinkle with the Parmesan cheese and then the olives. Top the entire quiche with mozzarella cheese. Bake at 375F for 35-45 minutes or until firm.

Chicken Crêpes
Yield: 24-26 crêpes
1½ cups flour
¼ teaspoon salt
6 eggs, well beaten
1²/₃ cups milk
3 tablespoons melted shortening

Combine flour and salt. Combine eggs, milk and shortening. Add flour mixture to egg mixture and beat until smooth. Pour ¼ cup batter onto a hot, lightly greased griddle or crêpe pan to make a crêpe of 4-5 inches in diameter. With the bottom of the measuring cup spread out the batter to make a thin crêpe or tip the pan to make the crêpe as thin as possible. When one side is brown, flip the crêpe to brown the other side. Cool.

Chicken Filling for Crêpes
Yield: filling for 24-26 crêpes

4-6 ounce boneless, skinless (each)
  chicken breasts, cooked
1 tablespoon olive oil or butter
1 cup celery, diced
1 cup red bell pepper, diced
1 cup sliced mushrooms
1 bunch green onions with tops,
  chopped
2 teaspoons minced garlic
1 teaspoon Lawry's® seasoned salt
1 teaspoon Beau Monde
2 teaspoons dill weed
1 teaspoon white pepper
2-14.5 ounce cans (each) chicken broth
1 cup evaporated milk
1¼ cups water
½ cup cornstarch
¼ cup white cooking wine
no-stick baking spray

Sauté celery, red bell peppers, mushrooms, onions and garlic in olive oil. In a large saucepan, mix the chicken broth and evaporated milk together and bring to a boil. Mix cornstarch and water and whisk until the sauce is thickened to a nice consistency. Add the chicken, vegetables and spices and heat thoroughly. Add the wine and cook for a few more minutes until the sauce is bubbly. Lay out the crêpes on the countertop. Place ¼ cup of the chicken mixture down the center of each crêpe and fold each side over to make a rolled crêpe. Spray 2-9x13 pans. Place crêpes into pans. Bake for 10-15 minutes before serving time. Serve crêpes hot without gravy or with gravy on the side.

Gravy to Serve with Crêpes
Yield: 24-26 servings

2-14.5 ounce cans (each) chicken broth
1 cup evaporated milk
1 tablespoon butter
1¼ cups water
¼ cup cornstarch
½ cup water
1 teaspoon white pepper
2 teaspoons dill weed
1 teaspoon Beau Monde
2 tablespoons white wine

Combine broth, milk, butter and seasonings. With a wire whip, combine the water and cornstarch to make a smooth consistency. Bring the broth mixture to a boil and slowly add the cornstarch mixture to thicken the gravy. Stir in the wine and simmer on low stirring constantly for a few minutes. Serve with the crêpes.

Tip
If you do not want to make crêpes due to lack of time, substitute the chicken crêpes with Chicken a la King. Make the chicken filling for the crêpes and serve over rice or egg noodles. You can also serve it over ready-made biscuits or biscuits that have been baked from a can to save time.

Fresh Strawberries and Cantaloupe Platter
Yield: 20 servings

1 cantaloupe
2 pints fresh strawberries
1 bunch parsley

Peel cantaloupe. Cut in half. Cut each half into 10 long thin wedges. Arrange on a 12-inch tray. Clean strawberries and dry. Leave the hull on each strawberry. Neatly arrange strawberries on the platter with cantaloupe. Serve chilled with the main course.

Ham, Cheese and Grape Platter
Yield: 20 servings

20 slices deli ham
8 slices Swiss cheese
⅓ pound green grapes
⅓ pound red grapes
6 strawberries
Roll each slice of ham up like a diploma. Cut each slice of cheese into four pieces. Clean the grapes and cut into small clumps. Clean the strawberries. Dry the grapes and strawberries with a paper towel. Place the cheese at the end of the tray and arrange two rows of ham. Garnish with grapes and strawberries.
Serve with cocktail buns.

Cocktail Buns
Yield: 20 servings

8 white cocktail buns
8 wheat cocktail buns
8 rye cocktail buns
1 green cloth dinner napkin
Slice the buns with a hinge. Arrange the buns in a basket lined with a napkin.

Condiments
Yield: 20 servings

1 small bowl whipped butter
1 small bowl mustard
1 small bowl mayonnaise

Place ½ pound butter into a mixing bowl. Beat butter until smooth. Place whipped butter into a bowl. Place mustard and mayonnaise into small bowls.
Serve with the ham and cheese platter.

Cornbread Hearts
Yield: 48 cornbread hearts

2-8 ounce boxes (each)
  Jiffy® corn muffin mixes
2 eggs

Cornbread Hearts, continued

²/₃ **cup milk**
no-stick baking spray
2 heart shaped muffin pans
1-12 inch doily

Place cornbread mixes into a bowl. Add eggs and milk. Spray no-stick baking spray into the mini heart shape muffin tins. Add a little less than 1 tablespoon of cornbread mix to each heart shaped muffin. Bake at 375F for about 10-12 minutes or until golden brown. Place heart shape muffins on a tray lined with a doily.

Tip

The orange coffee cake is made in a long narrow pan. Scandinavians used this pan to make Scandinavian Almond Cake. To make orange food coloring, add 2 drops yellow and 2 drops red food color.

Orange Coffee Cake
Yield: one coffee cake
           (18 slices)

1 cup sugar
1 egg
1 teaspoons orange flavoring
1 teaspoon orange zest
½ teaspoon cinnamon
²/₃ cup evaporated milk
1½ cups flour
1½ teaspoons baking powder
½ cup (1 stick) butter, melted
no-stick baking spray

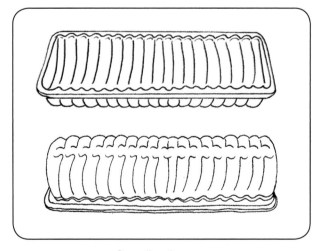

Scandinavian pan

Beat together the sugar, egg, orange flavoring, orange zest, cinnamon and milk. Add the flour and the baking powder and beat. Stir in the butter and beat until the batter is smooth. Pour batter into lightly greased Scandinavian pan with no-stick baking spray. Bake at 350F for 35-45 minutes or until toothpick in the center of the cake comes out clean. Edges must be golden brown. Cool 8 minutes in pan before removing. The cake will break if removed too soon. Sprinkle with powdered sugar while warm or spread orange glaze over the top of the coffee cake.

Orange Glaze
Yield: glaze for 1 orange coffee cake

1 cup powdered sugar
½ teaspoon orange flavoring
¼ teaspoon salt
2 tablespoons water
1-5x14 inch oblong doily
  (made from 10x14 folded doily)
orange food coloring
⅓ cup chopped pecans, optional
4 green maraschino cherries, drained

Orange Coffee Cake

Mix together the powdered sugar, orange flavoring, salt, food coloring and water until smooth. Turn coffee cake onto a cookie sheet. Spread glaze over the top and sides of the coffee cake while still warm. Sprinkle pecans over the top of the glazed coffee cake. Garnish with green maraschino cherries. Cool thoroughly. Fold doily in half and cut in half lengthwise. Line the 5x16 inch tray with half of the doily. Transfer the coffee cake onto the serving tray. (See illustration above).

 Dessert Menu (refer to pages 4 for illustration of dessert items)

Bridal Shower Cake
Yield: 10 servings

1-18.25 ounce fudge
  marble cake
1¼ cups water
⅓ cup canola oil
3 eggs
no-stick baking spray
3-10 inch round cardboard
  cake circles
1 small bouquet orange
  silk flowers
6-8 silk ferns
1 bride figure
1 miniature green umbrella

Bridal Shower Cake

Preheat oven to 350F. Spray 3-9 inch round cake pans with no-stick baking spray. Follow directions on cake mix box. Divide the batter among 3-9 inch baking pans. Bake for 20-25 minutes or until toothpick in the middle comes out clean. Cool on cooling racks for 10 minutes. Turn cake out onto 3 different foiled round cardboard cake circles. Make butter cream frosting and decorate cake. (See illustration on page 14).

Butter Cream Frosting
Yield: frosts one 9-inch cake

1 cup butter, softened
1 cup shortening
2 pounds powdered sugar
1 teaspoon vanilla
⅓ cup water
½ teaspoon salt

In a five quart mixing bowl, beat butter and shortening together. Alternate the water with the powdered sugar. Add the vanilla and salt and continue to beat the frosting until smooth and creamy. Leave the first layer of cake on the foiled cardboard. Frost the layer and remove second layer off cardboard and place on the first layer of cake. Repeat. Frost the top and sides of the cake. Smooth frosted cake with spatula that has been dipped into hot water. Place the bride figure in the center of the cake. Arrange flowers around the bride figure. Using a number 30 cake decorating tip, pipe on top and bottom borders and also around the bottom of the bride figure. Place the umbrella to the left side of the cake. (See page 19 for the napkin detail and umbrella pattern).

Chocolate Chip Cherry Flan Torte
Yield: 2-10 inch flan tortes

1-18.25 ounce dark chocolate
  cake mix
1¼ cup water
⅓ canola oil
3 eggs
1 cup chocolate chips
2-21 ounce cans (each)
  cherry pie filling, divided

Chocolate Chip Cherry Flan Torte, continued

2-12 ounce containers (each)
  non-dairy whipped topping
no-stick cooking spray
2-10 inch cardboard circles lined with foil

Preheat oven to 350F. Add water, oil and eggs to cake mix. Beat until smooth. Spray 2-10 inch flan torte pans with no-stick cooking spray. Divide the cake batter between the two pans. Bake for 20 minutes or until toothpick in the middle comes out clean. Cool for 3-5 minutes and remove from the pan. Place each flan cake onto a foiled cardboard circle. Place each cake onto a footed 12-inch cake plate. When thoroughly cooled and using a number 1C cake decorating tip, fill in the cavity of the torte with the non-dairy whipped topping and also a border around the topside of each flan torte. Sprinkle chocolate chips over the whipped topping per cake. Place one can of cherry pie filling around the outside of the torte per torte.

 Beverages

Orange Sherbet Punch
Yield: 20 servings

1 gallon Hawaiian® orange
  ocean drink
1-2 liter bottle Sprite®
1-16 ounce can crushed pineapple
2 pints orange sherbet
1 lime, sliced

In a large punch bowl, mix together half of the orange ocean drink, half of the Sprite® and 1 can of crushed pineapple with juice. Float scoops of sherbet in the punch and garnish with lime slices.

Coffee, Tea and Milk Detail

See chart in the Fallen in Love chapter on page 188 for making the right portions of coffee. One gallon of milk is more than enough milk for a crowd of twenty. Many people will not drink milk; they will enjoy the punch and coffee. Fill the teapot with water and bring to a boil. Remove from the stove. Place a small tray lined with tea bags and let the guests help themselves.

How to Lay Out the Buffet Table
(The Menu from Left to Right):

1. **Punch**
2. **Cornbread Hearts**
3. **Orange Coffee Cake**
4. **Plain Bread**
5. **Cocktail Rolls**
6. **Ham and Cheese Tray**
7. **Butter, Mustard and Mayonnaise**
8. **Chicken Crêpes**
9. **Orange Juice and Ice**
10. **Ripe Olive Quiche**
11. **Broccoli Quiche**
12. **Fresh Strawberries and Cantaloupe Platter**
13. **Chocolate Chip Cherry Flan Torte**
14. **Bridal Shower Cake**

Serve the coffee, tea, cream and sugar in the kitchen.

How to Set Up the Guest Tables
Yield: 6 per table

Each place setting has the following setup:
Starting left to right

One cloth napkin with napkin ring adorned with shower umbrella in green, a dinner fork, knife (blade away from spoon), spoon, water glass above the tip of the knife and a dessert fork centered and above the dinner plate. Each guest receives a game in a bag at her place setting. (See picture on page 5).

Umbrella Decoration Napkin Ring Detail

12 napkin rings
2-8x11 sheets light weight green cardboard
1 yard green ribbon (3 inches wide)
1 yard yellow gold ribbon (¾ inch wide)
1 yard orange ribbon (¼ inch wide

Follow the steps with directions on page 19 on how to assemble the umbrella decoration napkin ring detail. At the guest table, on the day of the party, place one umbrella napkin ring at each guest's place setting (next to the fork with the umbrella facing up).

Use this same pattern for making umbrellas for both the napkin rings and the shower cake.

Umbrella Pattern

The length of the umbrella is approximately 4¼ inches long. The lace on the green umbrella is 1½ inches wide and 3 inches long.

Details on the Ribbon:

It is one layer of green ribbon 3 inches wide with one layer of yellow ribon ¾ inches wide. There is an orange ribbon going down the center of the yellow ribbon and the orange ribbon is ¼ inch wide. Basically the peak of the umbrella sticks out and the remainder of the top of the umbrella is covered by the ribbon. The umbrella is then glued on to the wooden napkin ring.

fig.1
The size of the umbrella used to make the napkin. Trace and cut out the umbrellas.

Umbrella Decoration Napkin Ring Detail, continued

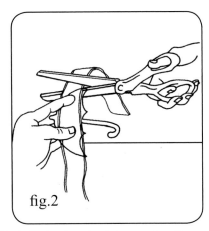

fig.2

Cut ribbons to fit umbrellas.

fig.3a

fig.3b

fig.3c

Layer and glue down the green ribbon on the umbrella.

Glue the yellow gold down the center of the green ribbon.

Glue the orange ribbon down the center of the yellow gold ribbon.

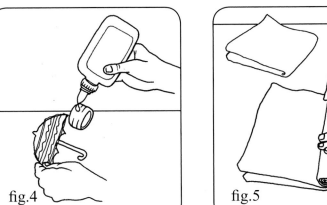

fig.4

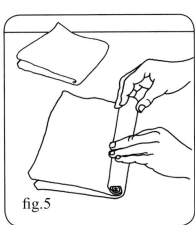

fig.5

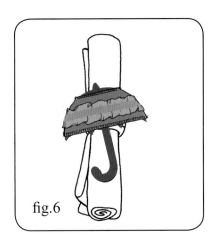

fig.6

Glue umbrella to napkin ring.

Roll the napkin like a diploma.

Place napkin through the napkin ring.

Game in a Bag

The game in the bag has one or two packets of seeds or a prop to help each guest think of some advice to give to the couple. Each place setting has a pen and a note card. Each guest has to write a note using the word or words on the package or jar or an item in the bag. The guest gives the bride-to-be wisdom of advice to have a good marriage and wish the happy couple best wishes for a good married life. Each guest can keep the bag.

Game in a Bag

Some of the cards stated as follows:

1. Lettuce and squash packets in one bag: "Lettuce" never be apart and "squash" any bad feelings. May your love continue to grow and flower into a beautiful garden. Don't let marriage squash your dreams (lettuce and squash).

2. Enjoy the warmth of love by sharing a cup of chicken noodle soup. Use your noodle and you will keep your love alive (chicken noodle soup).

3. Berry shower gel will keep your honeybee after you (berry shower gel).

4. Marriage isn't a snap but it works when two peas in a pod love each other (snap dragons and peas).

5. Let this bottle of glue keep you and your mate together in hard times. May your love be the glue that keeps you together forever and always. The glue often keeps the hard times from tearing you apart (glue).

6. Love is like a flower. Plant the seed and watch it grow in all the years ahead in your marriage. Add a little glue and scotch tape to always stick together. Always be sweet to each other and mix together your efforts to make a successful marriage (glue and scotch tape).

7. Start each day with a big smile and a warm heart. Have a soft heart toward each other (heart).

8. May this sanitizer kill the entire germ that invades on loving thoughts. It is 100% guaranteed that your marriage will be challenging, yet rewarding and happy most of the time. I hope you will always enjoy each other in your marriage. I wish you much joy, health, and happiness in your marriage. Give each other a helping hand when in need and always be supportive of each other in good and bad times (sanitizer).

9. I hope that your life together is as sweet as the flowers in your Sweet William garden. Life can be sweet with the brightness of each day. May you grow and bloom as a married couple. (Sweet William).

10. Keep track of your happy thoughts. These are perfect for leaving sweet notes to each other. Always be a honey to each other and be each other's keeper for the best interest of you as a couple (honey).

11. Put a little spice in your life and have fun doing simple things together to create beautiful memories (cinnamon and spice).

12. May you always shower each other with love (shower cap).

13. I know you two will stick together through thick and thin (popsicle sticks). (They were glued together and had a bride and groom painted on them).

The above are just a few of the examples for the game in a bag.

The guests had a good time writing and reading their notes to the bride. She too was very happy for the guests' good wishes.

It was interesting to listen to each guest talk about marriage and family life.

After the game we served dessert and opened gifts. The shower was well received by the guests. I also received many thank you notes for a job well done. The best thank you note of warm appreciation came from the bride-to-be.

The week after the shower I learned that the bride to-be and her fiancé spent an hour in private going through the cards and talking over the importance of working together as a couple to ensure a happy life. Her fiancé told her that these cards also meant a great deal to him. (See game in a bag illustration on page 20).

To conclude, it was a delight to be a part of this shower knowing it was fun and a job well done!

A Watermelon Theme Menu

Appetizers
Hot and Sweet Pepper Relish
Club Crackers
Chili Dip with Tortilla Chips
Ham Pinwheels

Beverages
Assorted Sodas

Main Course
Meatloaf Burgers
Cheese Slices
Salmon Patty Burgers with Tartar Sauce
Hamburger Buns
Lettuce and Tomato Slices
Onion Slices
Pickles and Olives
Ketchup, Yellow Mustard
Dijon Mustard, Mayonnaise
Potato Chips
Watermelon Compote with Blueberry Garnish
Spinach Pasta Salad
with Champagne Wine Vinegar Dressing

Desserts
Watermelon Ice Cream Mold
Sugar Fan Cookies

Chapter 2
A Couples' Bridal Shower–Watermelon Theme

Tracey and Jon's Love Story

Tracey and Jon were on different culinary teams in a small class in culinary school. They often found themselves competing against each other. Tracey's team seemed to always take first place while Jon's team came in second. Jon gave Tracey a hard time and was not always very kind, but he did admire her spirit. Tracey was very attractive with sparkling green eyes and auburn hair which she wore up under her chef hat. She was tall and trim and had many social graces. She was well liked by her teammates. She grew up in a beautiful lakeside home and was a strong swimmer and enjoyed many sports. Her family had run a catering business since Tracey was eight years old and she had helped her family earn a livelihood. She was well versed on garnishing food and making it attractive. These skills made her very quick in food preparation and she knew how to speak to please the judges.

Jon recognized Tracey for her qualities, but wanted so much to just take first place and win instead of Tracey. Jon was tall and muscular and liked to eat. He had deep blue eyes, medium brown hair and broad shoulders. Tracey sometimes ribbed Jon when her team won. She told him he had broad shoulders and could take on the burden of losing to her team.

For the entire school year they continued to be competitive. The next school year Mr. Mitch, the instructor, decided to put Tracey and Jon on the same team. At first they protested and told Mr. Mitch it was a bad choice. Mr. Mitch said they needed to work together as a team. To Tracey and Jon's surprise, they began to communicate and work together, coming up with innovative and creative ideas. They not only took first place for their team, but also won the state competition.

In October Jon invited Tracey to a formal dance. At first she said no, but with a little coaxing, she agreed to go. When Jon saw Tracey, he immediately told her that she was beautiful. They had a nice time together and she learned that he had two left feet on the dance floor. Tracey had learned to dance in a class with all females and had taken the lead for every dance. They had a good laugh over Jon's two left feet. She was sorry for leading Jon and tried harder to follow his lead.

At the end of the year both graduated from chef school with high honors. Jon moved to Lake George, New York and Tracey continued working at her parents' catering service. Jon held a very responsible position and liked his job, but somehow he did not feel complete. He missed Tracey. He called and told her that he missed her and after the summer season he would take a few days off and visit her. She also missed him. Tracey's parents offered Jon a position when he returned home. Business was good and they felt that they could pay him a good salary. He wanted to think about it first before committing to the job. He returned to New York and finished his summer job. He was offered another job back home with a five star hotel. He felt that this position was better suited to his personality. He wasn't sure he would enjoy catering and declined Tracey's parents' offer.

Tracey and Jon continued to date and discovered that they were falling in love. In January after the Christmas rush, Jon proposed to Tracey. They planned a simple fall wedding.

Planning the Watermelon Theme Shower

Tracey's mom suggested a couple's shower at the lake. Tracey always liked watermelon designs and watermelon-shaped ice cream. Jon thought a couple's watermelon theme party at Tracey's parents' lakeside home would be fun. They could water ski, play volleyball and ride the pontoon boat after supper. Tracey's family's catering business specialized in picnics and the watermelon theme was a popular picnic supper. It was casual, easy to prepare and fun. The watermelon mold dessert always received rave reviews.

Early that summer, Tracey and Jon planned the menu and the family thought the watermelon theme was great. They decided to invite 9 other couples to celebrate. Her mom would cook for 20, which would include Tracy and Jon. Her mom always over cooked and could easily accommodate any other family members helping with the party.

Appetizer Menu (refer to pages 40 for illustration of appetizer items)

Hot and Sweet Pepper Relish Dip
Yield: 20 servings

1-16 ounce jar sweet and hot pepper relish
3-8 ounce packages (each) cream cheese, softened
1 cup sunflower seeds
6 endive leaves, washed and dried
6 strawberries
1-14 ounce box reduced fat
  club crackers

Beat cream cheese until smooth and creamy. Add the pepper relish and beat until blended well. Place into 10-inch decorative quiche serving dish. Sprinkle with sunflower seeds. Outline the dip around the edge of the bowl with the endive leaves. Garnish with fresh strawberries. Arrange crackers in a basket lined with red paper or cloth napkin. See illustration on page 40.

Tip

I like to serve red, white and blue tortilla chips. This multicolored blend can be purchased in 9-ounce bags at your supermarket.

Tip

For showmanship, line the brim of a watermelon styled garden hat with three red napkins and alternate the different colored tortilla chips. See illustration on page 40. Blue corn chips are also very tasty with the chili dip. Organic corn chips are sold in 9-ounce bags at your supermarket.

Chili Dip
Yield: 20 servings

1-8 ounce package cream cheese, softened
½ teaspoon chili powder
1 teaspoon cumin
3 cups Mexican cheese, divided
¾ cup salsa
1-14 ounce can black beans,
  drained and rinsed
1-14 ounce can crispy corn,
  drained and rinsed
1-14 ounce can black olives, sliced
1 tomato, seeded and diced
3 scallions with tops, chopped
1-14 ounce package multicolor
  tortilla chips
1-12 ounce package white
  corn scoop tortilla chips

Beat cream cheese. Add the chili powder and cumin and beat until blended together. Spread over the bottom of a decorative 12-inch pie pan. Sprinkle 1 cup of Mexican cheese over the cream cheese mixture. Gently spread the salsa over the cheese. Sprinkle with a second cup of Mexican cheese. Top with the crispy corn and black beans. Complete with the remaining Mexican cup of cheese. Garnish with black olives, diced tomatoes and scallions. Serve with the multicolor tortilla chips and white corn scoop tortilla chips. See illustration on page 40.

Tip
There are 15 slices of bread to a 16-ounce loaf of bread and 20 slices of bread to a 20-ounce loaf of bread. Each loaf has two crusts. Do not use the crusts. Sixty pinwheel sandwiches serve 20 people and 120 pinwheel sandwiches serve 40 people. I like to make up the full recipe for serving 20 people and use any extra filling as a dip with crackers.

Ham Pinwheels
Yield: 60 finger sandwiches

1-20 ounce loaf whole wheat
 bread
6 ounces almond cheese
 spread
½ cup butter or margarine, softened
4 ounces cream cheese
4 slices deli ham, diced
2 tablespoons finely diced celery
½ teaspoon dehydrated minced onion
2 teaspoons Dijon mustard
66 Craisins®
1 bunch cilantro
6 whole almonds
1-12 inch platter
1-12 inch doily

Ham Pinwheels
Yield: 120 finger sandwiches

2-16 ounce loaves (each) whole wheat
 bread
1-12 ounce container almond cheese
 spread
1 cup butter or margarine, softened
1-8 ounce package cream cheese
8 slices deli ham, diced
¼ cup finely diced celery
1 teaspoon dehydrated minced onion
1 tablespoon Dijon mustard
132 Craisins®
2 bunches cilantro
12 whole almonds
2-12 inch platters
2-12 inch doilies

Cut off the crusts on each slice of bread. With a rolling pin, flatten the bread. Butter each slice of bread. Set aside. Beat together the almond cheese spread and cream cheese until smooth and creamy. Add the ham, celery, onion and Dijon mustard. Stir all the ingredients until mixed together well. Spread each slice of bread with filling. Roll up into a diploma shape. Place sandwiches on a platter, cover and refrigerate overnight. Cut each sandwich into 4 pieces to form pinwheels. Place on a 12-inch platter lined with a doily. Garnish each center of the pinwheel with one Craisin®. Wash and dry the cilantro. Place the cilantro in middle of the platter. Garnish with the almonds and Craisins®. Also, place the cilantro in a circle in between the first and second pinwheel sandwiches. Wrap the tray(s) with plastic wrap; refrigerate until serving time.

 Beverages

Assorted Sodas
Yield: 30 Sodas

30 assorted sodas
10 pounds ice
1 large cooler

Place sodas in the cooler and ice. Let the guests help themselves to the beverages.

Tip

When I make meatloaf burgers for 20-24 people, I usually like to make them in smaller batches. Use two large bowls and add like ingredients to each bowl in an assembly line fashion. Meatloaf burgers can be made in advance and frozen. Thaw out one day ahead of the party. Two batches yield 28-7 ounce burgers. In the past I have found that most people will only take one burger when it is a large size piece of meat. I buy pasta seasoning and shallot pepper from Penzeys Spice Company. To substitute pasta seasoning and shallot pepper, use 1 teaspoon Italian seasoning, 1/2 teaspoon onion powder and 1/4 teaspoon white pepper. Sam's Club sells 40 quarter-pound hamburgers by the case if you do not wish to make meatloaf burgers. However, meatloaf burgers are very tasty and a real crowd pleaser.

Tip

Not every guest will want cheese on their burger. The griller can place a slice of cheese on the burger per the guest's request at the grill site.

 Main Course Menu (see illustration on page 41 for main course items)

Meatloaf Burgers
Yield: 14-7 ounce burgers

3¾ pounds ground sirloin meat
3 eggs
¾ cup milk
1 small onion, diced
1 tablespoon minced garlic
1 tablespoon Worcestershire sauce
2 tablespoons yellow mustard
¼ cup ketchup
1½ cups Italian bread crumbs
1 teaspoon salt
1 teaspoon pepper
2 teaspoons pasta seasoning
1 teaspoon shallot pepper, optional
14 hamburger buns

Chef at the Grill Cooking Meatloaf Burgers and Salmon Patties

Place meat in a large bowl. Add eggs, milk, onion, garlic, Worcestershire sauce, mustard, ketchup, Italian bread crumbs, salt, pepper, pasta seasoning and shallot pepper. Mix all ingredients together. Using a hamburger maker, form the mixture into fourteen 7-ounce patties. Place each patty into a sandwich bag. Place filled sandwich bags into a gallon size bag (6-8) per bag.

Freeze the burgers and take out the amount needed for serving family or guests. Grill burgers at 350F for 15 minutes, about 7½ minutes on each side. Place cheese slice on cooked burgers to order. Invite the guests to pick up their burger at the grill site. Place sliced hamburger buns in a large basket lined with two red cloth napkins. Serve buns on the main dinner buffet table. (See photo of griller and burgers on page 28).

Grocery List for Condiments and Meatloaf Burger Fixings
Yield: 16-20 servings

1-12 ounce package single slices
   American cheese
   (16 slices per package)
1-32 ounce jar dill pickle hamburger
   slices, drained
2-24 ounce jars (each) dill pickle
   spears, drained
1-16 ounce jar bread
   and butter pickles
1-6 ounce can black olives
4 medium tomatoes, sliced
3 medium onions, sliced
1 large head romaine lettuce
1-32 fluid ounce jar mayonnaise
1-36 ounce bottle ketchup
1-14 ounce container yellow mustard

Preparation and Presentation of Condiments and Meatloaf Burger Fixings

Place American cheese slices near the grill. Using 6 oval shaped dishes with watermelon pattern, place each of the following items in each dish: dill pickle slices, dill pickle spears, bread and butter pickles, black olives, tomato slices and onion slices. Clean romaine lettuce. Pat dry with paper towel. Using a scissors cut the center rib out of each leaf. Place the lettuce on a 9-inch glass plate. Place mayonnaise into a glass footed compote. Place ketchup, tartar sauce and mustard into small glass bowls. Place bowls onto a wooden condiment tray. Refill condiments as needed. Cover and refrigerate the fixings and condiments until just before serving. At serving time place the lettuce on the table. Arrange the dill pickle slices, bread and butter pickle slices, dill pickle spears, olives, tomatoes and onion filled dishes around the lettuce plate to form a sunburst. See illustration on page 41.

Tip

If you have guests that do not like any kind of fish, substitute turkey burgers for salmon patty burgers. See recipe on 31.

Salmon Patty Burgers
Yield: 8 quarter pound salmon patties

2-14 ounce cans (each) pink salmon,
  rinsed and drained
1 tablespoon dehydrated minced
  onion
1 tablespoon minced garlic
2 tablespoons freshly squeezed
  lemon juice
1 teaspoon black pepper
1/3 cup celery, diced
3 eggs, slightly beaten
2 teaspoons Tones® salmon
  and seafood seasoning
2 teaspoons horseradish sauce
2 drops Tabasco® sauce
1½ cups Italian breadcrumbs

Place salmon in a medium size bowl. Add onion, garlic, lemon juice, black pepper, celery, eggs, seafood seasoning, horseradish sauce, Tabasco® sauce and breadcrumbs. Mix all the ingredients together and form into eight 4-ounce balls. Flatten each ball out into a patty. Place each patty into a sandwich bag. Refrigerate and grill on the day of the party.

Tip

Almost every guest will put tartar sauce on a salmon patty. I like homemade tartar sauce. Make salmon patties one day ahead of time and refrigerate overnight for best results.

Tartar Sauce
Yield: 8 servings

1¼ cups mayonnaise
1 tablespoon freshly squeezed lemon
  juice
¼ teaspoon Worcestershire sauce
2 drops Tabasco® sauce, optional
2 teaspoons dill pickle relish

Tartar Sauce
Yield: 16 servings

2½ cups mayonnaise
2 tablespoons freshly squeezed lemon
  juice
½ teaspoon Worcestershire sauce
3 drops Tabasco® sauce, optional
1 tablespoon dill pickle relish

Mix together the mayonnaise, pickle relish, lemon juice, Worcestershire sauce and Tabasco® sauce in a small bowl. Serve in a small glass bowl. See illustration on page 41.

Turkey Burgers
Yield: 6 turkey burgers

1 pound extra lean ground turkey
1-¾ ounce package fresh basil,
  chopped (¼ cup)
¼ cup Kalamata olives, chopped
¼ cup celery, diced
¼ cup feta cheese, crumbled
1 tablespoon red onion, chopped fine
1 egg
1 teaspoon Greek seasoning
½ teaspoon salt
½ teaspoon pepper
⅓ cup Italian style bread crumbs

In a medium size bowl, mix together turkey, basil, olives, celery, feta cheese, red onion, egg, Greek seasoning, salt, pepper and bread crumbs. Shape into 6 turkey burgers. Cook the turkey burgers on the grill. Serve on a bun.

Potato Chips
Yield: 20 servings

2-1 pound bags (each)
  potato chips

Arrange potato chips in a bowl. Serve potato chips as an appetizer and also with the main meal.

Watermelon Compote with Blueberry Garnish
Yield: 20 servings

1 large watermelon, cut into
  small chunks
1 honeydew melon
1 pint blueberries
1 bunch parsley, cleaned

Place small watermelon chunks in a large oval watermelon patterned bowl. Make the melon balls from the honeydew melon. Stir the watermelon and melon balls together. Garnish with blueberries and parsley sprigs. Serve with the main course.

Spinach Pasta Salad
Yield: 20 servings

1-16 ounce box penne pasta
¼ cup olive oil
1 teaspoon salt
1-16 ounce package fresh
  flat leaf spinach
1-5 ounce package spring mix
1 pint grape tomatoes, washed
  dried and divided
1-14 ounce can quartered artichoke
  hearts, drained and chopped
2 cups feta cheese, diced and
  divided
1 cup pine nuts
1-6 ounce can large pitted
  ripe olives, drained
½ thinly sliced medium red onion

Champagne Wine Vinegar Dressing

½ cup champagne
  wine vinegar
6 tablespoons water
1 cup olive oil
2-0.7 packages (each)
  Good Seasons®
  salad dressing mix

Garnish for Spinach Pasta Salad

1 head romaine lettuce
½ cup feta cheese
½ cup grape tomatoes

Add cold water to a large stockpot. Add 1 teaspoon salt. Bring water to a boil. Add the penne pasta. Cook until tender. Drain in colander. Rinse the penne pasta with cold water. Dab the pasta dry with a paper towel. Place cooked pasta in a large bowl. Wash the spinach; cut off the tails of each spinach leaf. Wash the spring mix. Dab the spinach and spring mix dry with paper towel. Add to the pasta, and mix in 1 cup grape tomatoes, artichoke hearts, 1½ cups feta cheese, pine nuts, olives and red onions. Set the salad aside.

In a medium size stainless steel bowl, whisk together the vinegar, water, olive oil and the Good Seasons® salad dressing mix. Pour over the salad and toss ingredients until well coated. Wash each individual romaine lettuce leaf. Dry with paper towel. Line the pasta serving bowl with the romaine lettuce leaves and fill with pasta salad. Garnish with remaining feta cheese and grape tomatoes.

Tip

Bombe pans are often sold on e-Bay. My friend, Glen, lends out his bombe pan to our circle. This watermelon ice cream mold gets every guest's attention as each serving looks just like a slice of watermelon. It is so easy to make and very refreshing after a hardy meal. The sugar fan cookie adds to the watermelon ice cream mold dessert and also tops off a great dessert for a touch of showmanship.

Desserts (see illustration on page 42 for dessert items)

Watermelon Ice Cream Mold
Yield: 10 slices per mold

1 oval bombe pan with lid (fig.1a)
  or 1 rounded stainless steel bowl (fig.1b)
2 sheets plastic wrap
2 pints vanilla ice cream, divided
¾ quart strawberry ice cream
1 cup miniature chocolate chips
green food coloring
red food coloring

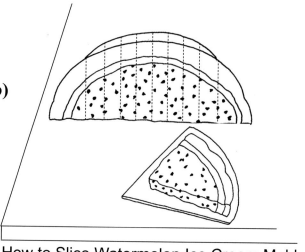

How to Slice Watermelon Ice Cream Mold.

Detailed Directions

Line the bombe pan with plastic wrap (fig.2). If you do not have a bombe pan use a rounded stainless steel bowl (fig.1b) and follow the same directions as using the bombe pan. Freeze the bombe mold for two hours. Soften 1 pint vanilla ice cream. Scoop the ice cream into a large mixing bowl (fig.3). Add 4 to 5 drops of green food coloring. Beat the ice cream until the green color is consistent throughout. Spread a thin layer of green ice cream into the bombe pan to cover the entire surface in the mold (fig.4). Place lid over the container and freeze the ice cream overnight. Soften a second pint of vanilla ice cream. Beat the vanilla ice cream to have a smooth consistency. Place a thin layer of vanilla ice cream over the green ice cream (fig.5). Cover and freeze the mold again overnight. Soften the strawberry ice cream. Add the red food coloring to the strawberry ice cream to create the same color as the flesh of a watermelon. Mix together ice cream and food coloring until food coloring is evenly distributed. Stir the chocolate chips into the ice cream. Fill the cavity of the bombe pan with the strawberry ice cream (fig.6). Cover and freeze overnight. On the day of the party, just before serving time, take the watermelon dessert out of the mold (fig.7). Remove the plastic wrap. Place a very sharp knife into a pitcher of boiling water. Slice the watermelon ice cream crosswise into 10 slices (fig.8). Continue to slice the pieces in a crosswise fashion; place one slice of ice cream on chilled watermelon design plates and serve immediately. For larger crowds, slice and plate up watermelon ice cream ahead of time; store in the freezer until serving time. (See line drawing with step by step directions on page 35).

Watermelon Ice Cream Mold, continued

Line Drawing Steps for Making the Watermelon Icecream Mold in the Bombe Pan and Stainless Steel Rounded Bowl (Fig. 1-8)

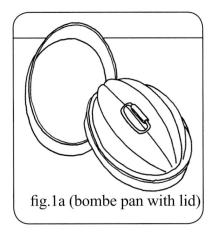

fig.1a (bombe pan with lid)

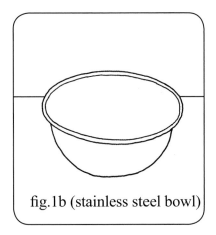

fig.1b (stainless steel bowl)

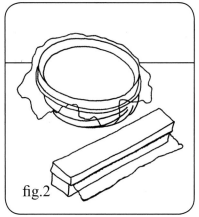

fig.2

Line pan with plastic wrap.

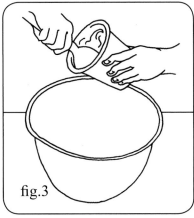

fig.3

Place softened ice cream into bombe pan; add the food green and blend.

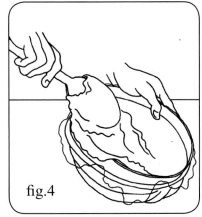

fig.4

Place a thin layer of green ice cream into bombe pan. Freeze overnight.

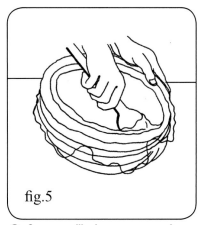

fig.5

Soften vanilla ice cream; place a thin layer over the green ice cream. Freeze overnight.

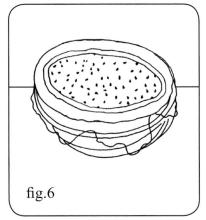

fig.6

Soften strawberry ice cream; Blend in chocolate chips. Fill cavity with ice cream. Freeze overnight.

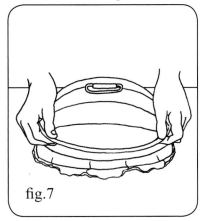

fig.7

Unmold ice cream and remove plastic wrap.

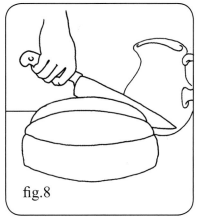

fig.8

Cut into slices and serve on plates.

Sugar Fan Cookies
Yield: 75 fan cookies

2/3 cup shortening
¾ cup granulated sugar
1 egg
2 tablespoons milk
½ teaspoon grated orange peel
½ teaspoon vanilla
2 cups flour
1½ teaspoons baking powder
¼ teaspoon salt
parchment paper
raw sugar
red decorating sugar
parchment paper

Sugar Fan Cookies
Yield: 150 fan cookies

1⅓ cups shortening
1½ cups granulated sugar
2 eggs
¼ cup milk
1 teaspoon grated orange peel
1 teaspoon vanilla
4 cups flour
3 teaspoons baking powder
½ teaspoon salt
parchment paper
raw sugar
red decorating sugar
parchment paper

Detailed Directions for Assembling Fan Cookies

Cream together the shortening, sugar, egg, orange peel and vanilla. Stir in the milk. In a separate bowl, mix together flour, baking powder and salt. Slowly add the flour mixture to the shortening and egg mixture and beat until mixed together well. Add green food coloring to ¼ of the dough. Chill each dough in two separate bowls for at least one hour. On a floured board, roll out the dough ¼ inch thick. Using a 4-inch round cookie cutter, cut out the cookie rounds (fig.1). Cut each round in half lengthwise and then crosswise to form 4 fan shaped cookies, even in size (fig.2). Using a fork, lightly press the fork down around the top edges of each cookie to form a decorative design (fig.3). Gently run a table knife from the rounded end of the cookie to the tip to make six lines as on a fan. Do not cut through the cookie (fig.4). Sprinkle raw sugar on 3 dozen green cookies, red sugar on 4 dozen cookies and raw sugar on the remaining white fan cookies. Cut parchment paper to fit the cookie sheet. Place the cookies on the lined cookie sheet (fig.5). Bake at 375F for 10-12 minutes or until lightly golden brown. Cool cookies on cooling rack. Arrange the cookies on a glass mirror and serve with the watermelon shaped ice cream slices. (See figure 1-5 on page 37 for general directions).

Line Drawing Steps for Making the Sugar Fan Cookies (Fig. 1-5)

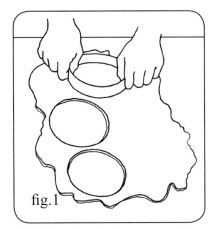

Cut out cookies

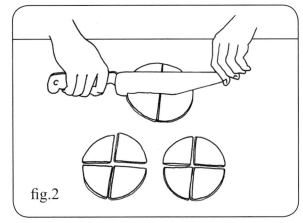

Cut each cookie into 4 pieces

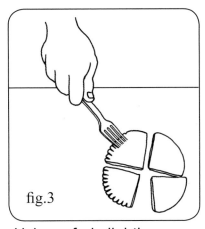

Using a fork, lightly press the fork down around the top edges of each cookie.

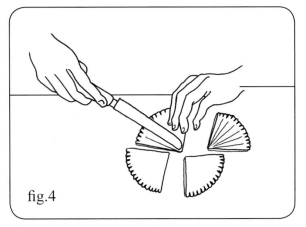

Gently run a table kinfe from the rounded end of the cookie to make six lines as on a fan.

fig.5
Sprinkle raw sugar over fan cookies.

Napkin Detail Steps (Fig. 1-5)

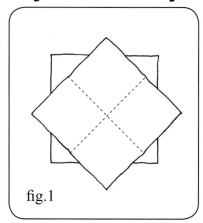

fig.1

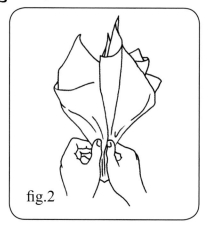

fig.2

Place an unfolded red napkin on the table and crisscross an unfolded green napkin over the red napkin.

Pinch the napkin stacked together (2-4 inches) up from the bottom.

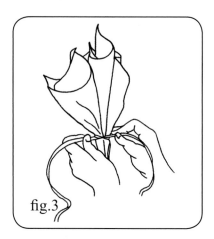

fig.3

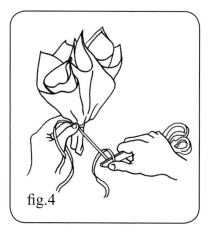

fig.4

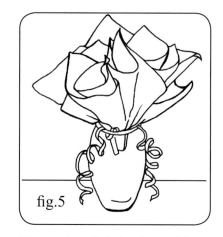

fig.5

Tie off 33 inches of brown curling ribbon to form a bouquet.

Curl the two ribbon ends.

Place the finished napkin into the glass and let the ribbon hang over the sides of the glass.

Guests will take their basket to the buffet table. Each basket is covered with plastic wrap.

The picture shown is a set up for 8 guests. Tracey suggested using 8-foot tables since they had green tablecloths that looked like the lines of the watermelon to fit the tables. She also had the watermelon shaped baskets, red silverware, green glasses and red and green napkins to make a great table setting. She had the local florist arrange the flowers in a watermelon design pitcher.

The Guest Table Setup
Yield: one guest table of 8

1. Place the green striped tablecloth on the 8-foot table.
2. Place one watermelon design basket at each place setting.
3. Place a fork to the left of the basket, a knife to the right of the basket and the spoon to the right of the knife.
4. Place a glass above the tip of the knife with napkin bouquet in each glass.
5. Place the watermelon pitcher bouquet in the center of the table.

Guest Table Setup

The Appetizer Table

1. Cover the 8-foot table with the green striped material.
2. Place the watermelon centerpiece at the end of the appetizer table. Place the two trays of pinwheel sandwiches above the centerpiece (one on the right side and the other on the left side of the buffet table with the plates in between the pinwheel sandwiches).
3. Place the watermelon design hat with assorted tortilla chips above the plates and slightly left on the table with napkins to the right of the tortilla chips.
4. Place the chili dip across from the tortilla chips.
5. Place the basket of crackers above the chili dip.
6. Place the potato chips to the left of the crackers.
7. Place the pepper relish dip above the crackers.
8. Place extra plates and napkins at the end of the line on the 8-foot table.

Appetizer Table Setup

The Buffet Table with the Main Course

1. Cover the 8-foot table with a green striped tablecloth.
2. Place the basket of buns at the end of the table.
3. Place the centerpiece slightly to the left of the roll basket.
4. Place the spinach pasta salad above the centerpiece.
6. Place the watermelon salad to the left of the spinach salad.
7. Place the lettuce in the middle of the sunburst.
8. Place three containers of pickles, tomatoes, onions and black olives around the lettuce to form the sunburst. Place the mayonnaise, slightly left of the other condiments and next to the dill pickle slices.
9. Place the tray with ketchup, tartar sauce and mustard at the end of the buffet table.
10. Place extra napkins across from the tray with the ketchup, tartar sauce and mustard. (The fork helps to hold the napkins in place.)

Main Course Table Setup

The Dessert Table

Dessert Table Setup

1. Cover the 8-foot table with the green striped tablecloth.
2. Place the arranged cookies in the center of the table.
3. Place the plates of ice cream along each side of the cookies.
4. Place the centerpiece to the left end side of the plated ice cream.
5. Place napkins at the far end of the buffet table. (See picture on this page).

Serving Pieces Needed for Appetizer Table

1. Hot and sweet pepper relish dip—2 serving spoons
2. Chip dip—2 serving spoons
3. Ham pinwheel sandwiches—two small tongs

Serving Pieces Needed for the Main Course Table

1. The chef will need two spatulas (one for the burgers and one for the salmon patties).
2. Use two half pans with covers to help keep the meat hot.
3. Buns—2 tongs
4. Watermelon with blueberry garnish—2 tongs
5. Spinach pasta salad—2 tongs
6. Lettuce—1 tong
7. Tomatoes—1 tong
8. Onions— 1 tong
9. Pickles—3 tongs (one tong for each dish of pickles)
10. Mayonnaise—1 spoon
11. Ketchup—1 small spoon
12. Tartar sauce—1 small spoon
13. Mustard—1 small spoon

Serving Pieces Needed for Dessert Table

Cookies are finger foods—none.
Place one spoon per watermelon ice cream serving.

Enjoy your picnic shower!!!

An Open House Engagement Party Menu

Lemon Lime Punch

Pink Champagne

Ham Salad Finger Sandwiches

Chicken Tartlets

Radish Rose Tree with

Stuffed Celery

Stuffed Dates and

Strawberry Platter

Wedding Bell Cheese Dip

with Crackers

Flying Flamingo Pineapple Cheese Tree

Shrimp Cocktail with Shrimp Sauce

Dilly Tomato Finger Sandwiches

Mixed Nuts

Chapter 3
An Open House Engagement and Bridal Shower Theme

Appetizers are often served at an open house with a champagne toast for an engagement and bridal shower combination. The engaged couple would be the focus at the open house. Guests would come in and visit with the couple. They present their gift and toast the couple with a glass of champagne if so desired. Guests go through the buffet line and help themselves to the appetizers. The cold appetizer buffet is easy to prepare a day ahead of time. Set out the food 45-60 minutes before serving time. Sometimes a ½ sheet cake is made and served at the bridal shower. Others prefer to have tea cookies and finger desserts served at a separate table in addition to the appetizers.

Appetizer Setup

Appetizer Setup, continued

Punch Setup

Pink Champagne
Yield: 6 glasses

1 bottle pink champagne

Chill the champagne. Pour the champagne for guests as needed. Have an extra bottle chilling in the ice bucket.

Tip
Use salad dressing for sweeter tasting dressing and a good quality mayonnaise for a lesser sweet tasting ham salad or use half of each style of dressing. Ham salad can be purchased in the deli department at a local grocery store.

Ham Salad Finger Sandwiches
Yield: 40 finger sandwiches

1 pound cooked ham, ground
2 tablespoons sweet pickle relish
⅓ cup celery, diced
1 tablespoon yellow mustard
1 teaspoon Worcestershire sauce
1 teaspoon minced garlic
2 teaspoons dehydrated onion
½ cup salad dressing
1 loaf cocktail pumpernickel bread
½ cup butter or margarine, softened
1-6 ounce can large ripe olives, drained
1-12 inch round serving tray
1-12 inch doily

Ham Salad Finger Sandwiches

Mix together the ham, pickle relish, celery, mustard, Worcestershire sauce, garlic, dehydrated onion and moisten with salad dressing. Butter each slice of bread. Spread ham salad over each slice of bread. Place doily on a tray. Cut each ham salad sandwich in half to form a triangle. Place sandwiches on a tray. Clean and dry the parsley. Cut olives in half lengthwise and dry. Garnish with parsley and one half olive. (See photo above).

There are 15 filo shells per 1.90 ounce box. Make the chicken salad one day ahead of the shower. If filo shells are filled a day before of the party, the filo shells will become soft and soggy.

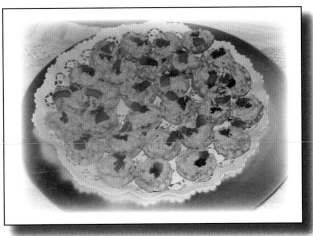

Chicken Tarlets

Chicken Tartlets
Yield: 3 dozen

3 boxes 1.90 ounce (each) filo shells
1-13 ounce can 98% fat free
 premium chicken breast in water
½ cup celery, finely diced
½ teaspoon white pepper
2 teaspoons dehydrated onion
1 teaspoon curry powder
¾ cup mayonnaise
½ bunch parsley
½ red bell pepper
1 doily

Chicken Tartlets
Yield: 5 dozen

4 boxes 1.90 ounce (each) filo shells
2-13 ounce cans (each) 98% fat free
 premium chicken breast in water
¾ cup celery, finely diced
¾ teaspoon white pepper
1 tablespoon dehydrated onion
2 teaspoons curry powder
1¼ cups mayonnaise
1 bunch parsley
1 red bell pepper
2 doilies

Drain and dry the chicken breast. Add the celery, white pepper, onion, garlic and curry powder. Moisten ingredients with the mayonnaise. Fill the filo tartlets with the chicken salad. Clean and dry the parsley. Cut red bell pepper into mini size squares to fit each tartlet. Garnish with parsley and red bell pepper. (See photo above).

Radish Rose Tree with Stuffed Celery

Yield: 24 radish roses
Yield: 36 stuffed celery

1-16 ounce package radishes
24 frilled toothpicks
1 grapefruit
1 sheet of foil
1-16 ounce package celery
1-5 ounce jar pimento spread
1-8 ounce package
  cream cheese, softened
1 teaspoon Worcestershire sauce
1 tablespoon finely chopped
  fresh chives
2 tablespoon Hormel® bacon bits
1-12 inch platter
1 head red leafy lettuce, cleaned paprika

Radish Rose Tree with Stuffed Celery

Cut the ends off of each radish. With a paring knife, form 5-6 petals on each radish. Place a toothpick from the bottom to the middle of each radish, half way up the radish. Wrap grapefruit with a sheet of foil. Place the grapefruit in footed compote. Stick each radish into the grapefruit at random. Weave small pieces of lettuce in between the radishes to complete the rose bush. Clean the celery. Dry and cut stalks of celery into 4 inch pieces. Place 36 celery pieces on a 12-inch platter lined with lettuce leaves. Set aside. Beat together pimento spread and cream cheese. Add Worcestershire sauce, chives and bacon bits. Continue to beat mixture until smooth. With a number 199 cake tube, pipe filling into the cavity of each piece of celery. Garnish with paprika. Cover and refrigerate. At serving time, place radish tree in footed compote in the center of the 12-inch tray. Place stuffed celery on the tray and around the radish tree. (See photo above).

Stuffed Dates and Strawberry Platter
Yield: 3 dozen dates and 2 quarts strawberries

1-2 pound container large dates
2-8 ounce packages (each)
  cream cheese, softened
1 tablespoon honey
1 teaspoon cinnamon
1 teaspoon sugar
2 drops pink food coloring
1-12 inch platter
1-12 inch doily

Stuffed Dates and Strawberry Platter

Cut each date halfway down. Cut opposite side half way down to form the tulip. Remove the pit. Mix together the cream cheese, honey, cinnamon, sugar and food coloring until smooth and creamy. With a number 30 cake tube, fill the center of each date flower. Place doily on a 12-inch plate. Clean and dry strawberries. On the outside row of the platter, alternate the date flowers with strawberries. Arrange the second row with the filled dates and fill in the center of the platter with strawberries. (See photo above).

Wedding Bell Cheese Dip with Crackers
Yield: 25-30 servings

1-8 ounce and 1-3 ounce
  package cream cheese
1-8 ounce block Danish
  Bleu cheese
¾ cups ripe olives,
  finely chopped or Craisins®
½ cup finely chopped pecans
¼ cup finely diced red pepper
1 teaspoon Worcestershire sauce
1-16 ounce box crackers
1-10 inch platter

Wedding Bell Cheese Dip with Crackers

Border
1-8 ounce package cream cheese
1 teaspoon Worcestershire sauce
½ teaspoon onion powder

Wedding Bell Dip with Crackers, continued

Garnish for Wedding Bell Dip
1 cup finely chopped pecans
1 radish slice
½ bunch parsley, cleaned

Beat 1-8 ounce block cream cheese and bleu cheese together. Add olives, pecans, red peppers and Worcestershire sauce. On a 10-inch platter, shape the cheese spread into a bell. For the border, beat 1-3 ounce cream cheese with the Worcestershire and onion powder until smooth. Using a number 28 cake tube, pipe border on the bell. Also, pipe on two lines across the lower part of the bell (about 1 inch apart). Sprinkle the pecans over the top of the cheese bell above and below the one inch mark. Place a radish slice in the middle of the bell ringer. Garnish with parsley. Serve with crackers. (See photo on page 49).

Tip

There are 20 flamingo stir sticks per package. There are 2 pieces of Colby Jack Cheese and 1 piece of string cheese per flamingo stir stick. Each Colby Jack stick is 5 inches long and each mozzarella string cheese is 4 inches long.

Flying Flamingo Pineapple Cheese Tree
Yield: 1 pineapple cheese tree

1 pineapple
50 flamingo stir sticks
2-10 ounce packages (each)
  Colby Jack sticks
1-12 ounce package mozzarella
  string cheese
1 head leafy red lettuce
2 pounds red seedless grapes
1-12 inch platter
1-16 ounce box crackers

Flying Flamingo PIneapple Cheese Tree

Place the whole pineapple with leaves on a 12 inch platter. Break off the ball on each flamingo stir stick. Leave ¾ inch at the bottom of each stir stick open so that it may be stuck into the flesh of the pineapple. Remove the plastic wrap from each string cheese and Colby Jack stick. Cut each Colby Jack cheese stick into 6 pieces and each mozzarella string cheese into 5 pieces. Slide the center of each piece of cheese through the flamingo stir stick, starting with the Colby cheese and alternating it with the mozzarella string cheese. At random and starting from top to bottom, insert the cheese filled flamingo stir sticks into the pineapple until all 50 cheese sticks have been placed into the pineapple. Clean and dry off the lettuce with a paper towel. Place leafy lettuce on platter around the pineapple tree. Clean and dry the grapes. With a scissors, cut the grapes into clumps of 3 or 4. Place the grapes onto the platter. Wrap the cheese tree with plastic wrap and refrigerate until serving time. Serve with crackers. (See photo on page 50).

Tip

One 32 ounce bag of frozen cleaned ready-to-serve shrimp has a 31-40 count. Figure 3 shrimp per person. Some will eat many shrimp and other guests will pass. For 50 people figure 150 shrimp or (5-32 ounce bags.)

Shrimp Cocktail with Shrimp Sauce
Yield: 30 people

3-32 ounce bags
  ready to serve shrimp
3 cups spring lettuce
1 lemon

Thaw the shrimp. Rinse the shrimp in cold water. Drain and dry each shrimp.

Shrimp Sauce
Yield: 30 servings

2-12 ounce bottles (each) chili sauce
1 tablespoon horseradish sauce
2 teaspoons Worcestershire sauce
1 teaspoon lemon juice

Shrimp Cocktail Platter

Whisk together the chili sauce, horseradish sauce, Worcestershire sauce and lemon juice. Divide the sauce into two bowls. Place one bowl in the center of the

A Drop-by Bridal Shower Menu

Peanut Butter Kisses
Mexican Wedding Cakes
Sweetheart Cookies
Romance Cookies
Chocolate No-Bake Cookies
Lucky Charms Cookies
Bridal Shower Horns
Lemon Poppy Seed Cookies
Bowls of Mixed Nuts and Mints
Chocolate Covered Pretzels
Yogurt Pretzels
Lemon Lime Punch

Chapter 4
A Drop-by Bridal Shower

Mark's Story

Jena and Mark met at a dance and became friends. The couple loved to dance and enjoyed their evenings together. They also liked to go to movies. After two years of courting, he hinted at getting married. He went to his hometown jewelers and purchased a diamond ring. When he returned, he invited her to a movie of her choice. He tucked the ring into his pants pocket. During the movie he placed his hand into his pocket only to find out that the ring was not there. He exclaimed, "Oh no!" He asked her to leave the movie. She had suspected that he was going to propose to her. After she left the theater he announced that he had lost the diamond. Could anyone around him help him find the diamond ring? He stated that he had blown his chance to get married by losing the ring. People began to crawl around the floor in the dark theater. Finally, a lady in the audience yelled, "I found it." He graciously thanked the lady and he left the theater. He then proposed to Jena. Upon his surprise, she accepted. Jena and Mark did not want to have a shower and they also wanted a very small wedding. However, her parents felt that a drop-by shower would be very appropriate. Some people may not know about a drop-by shower.

A drop-by shower is an open house that generally takes place for a 3-4 hour block in the afternoon. Generally, Saturday and Sunday are ideal days to have a drop-by shower. There are no games played at this style of shower. The guest is welcome to drop-by to present the bride a gift. The bride will open the gift and visit with the guest. The guest expresses her good wishes for a bright future upon the bride's wedding day. Some drop-by showers have a sweets table filled with assorted dainty small cookies or finger desserts, mints and nuts and also punch. Some drop-by showers also include a buffet table of cold finger appetizers. The guests can visit for a short while and then leave the shower. It is a great way to have a shower and less time consuming for the person giving the shower and also for the guests leading a very busy life. All the sweets served at the shower can be made in advance. Cookies can be frozen and thawed and arranged one day ahead of time. The hostess can make the buffet tables as simple or fancy as she so desires. She can use paper service or china. (See colored photos of the drop-by shower on pages 64-65).

Several family members, friends and neighbors volunteered to make the cookies. Jena's mom arranged the cookies on her beautiful milk white dishes and also arranged the tulip centerpiece.

Peanut Butter Kisses
Yield: 2½ dozen

½ cup butter, softened
½ cup peanut butter
¾ cup granulated sugar, divided
½ cup brown sugar
1 egg
1¼ cups flour
½ teaspoon baking powder
¾ teaspoon baking soda
¼ teaspoon salt
30 mini milk chocolate kisses

Peanut Butter Kisses

Preheat the oven to 375F. Mix together the butter, peanut butter, ½ cup sugar, brown sugar and egg until creamy. Mix together the flour, baking powder, baking soda and salt. Stir dry ingredients into the butter-sugar mixture. Roll the dough into small size balls. Place on a cookie sheet 3 inches apart on lightly greased baking sheet. Flatten with a fork by a crisscross per cookie. Sprinkle sugar over each cookie. Place a forefinger print in the middle of each cookie. Bake for 10-12 minutes. Remove cookies from the oven and place one mini kiss into the center of each cookie. Place each cookie on a cookie rack to cool. (See photo above).

Peanut Butter Kisses (variation)
Make a batch of peanut butter cookies. Omit the mini milk chocolate kisses. Add ½ cup of the mini pieces peanut butter candy in a crunch shell to the cookie mixture.

Mexican Wedding Cakes
Yield: 2½ dozen

1 cup butter, softened
1 cup powdered sugar, divided
1 teaspoon vanilla
2¼ cups flour

Mexican Wedding Cakes, continued

¼ teaspoon salt
¾ cup finely chopped walnuts

Mix together butter, ½ cup powdered sugar and vanilla. Add the flour, salt and walnuts. Stir ingredients until all ingredients hold together well. Roll into 1-inch balls. Place on ungreased baking sheet. Bake for 10-15 minutes. While still warm, roll in powdered sugar. Cool on cooking racks. (See photo on page 60 and 61).

Sweetheart Cookies
Yield: 5 dozen

1 cup butter, softened
1½ cup sugar
2 eggs
2 teaspoons orange flavoring
2¾ cups flour
2 teaspoons cream of tartar
1 teaspoon baking soda
¼ teaspoon salt

Sweetheart Cookies

Topping
⅓ cup sugar
½ teaspoon cinnamon
1-12 ounce jar strawberry preserves
1-12 ounce jar sweet orange marmalade

Preheat oven to 375F. Mix together the butter, sugar, eggs and orange flavoring. Stir in the flour, cream of tartar, baking soda and salt. Mix well. Mix together the sugar and cinnamon for the topping mixture. Roll the dough into ½ inch balls. Roll each cookie ball into the sugar cinnamon mixture. Place 2 inches apart on an ungreased baking sheet. Place a thumb print in the middle of each cookie. Place a small amount of strawberry preserves into the center of each cookie for half of the cookie dough and the sweet orange marmalade in the other half. Bake for 10-12 minutes. (These cookies will puff up at first, and then flatten out.) Cool for 1 minute and remove cookies from the baking sheet and cool on a cooling rack. (See photo above).

Romance Cookies
Yield: 24-28

½ cup butter, softened
¾ cup powdered sugar
1 tablespoon almond flavoring
1½ cups flour
dash of salt
food coloring
14 maraschino
  cherries, drained
42 mini milk chocolate kisses, (3 per cookie)

Romance Cookies

Frosting for Romance cookies
Yield: 40 cookies

1-16 ounce container
  chocolate frosting

Topping for Romance cookies
14 whole pecans
14 multi-colored
  chocolate decor

Pre-heat oven to 350F. Mix together the butter, powdered sugar, almond flavoring and food coloring of choice. Blend in flour and salt. Mix together well until dough can form a ball. Squeeze out excess liquid from each maraschino cherry. Wrap a level tablespoon of dough around the maraschino or 3 mini chocolate kisses. Place 1 inch apart on ungreased baking sheet. Bake 13-15 minutes. Cool 2 minutes. Remove from the baking sheet and cool thoroughly. Frost the top of each cookie and decorate with a pecan or multi-colored chocolate décor. (See photo above).

Chocolate No-Bake Cookies
Yield: 40

1-12 ounce package mini chocolate chips
3 cups chow mein noodles
1 cup whole cashew nuts

Chocolate No-Bake Cookies

Chocolate No-Bake Cookies, continued

40 pieces whole cashew nuts
½ cup Crasins®
40 mini foil baking cups
¼ cup butter, softened

Place chocolate chips in top of a double boiler over medium high heat. Stir chocolate chips until melted. Add the chow mein noodles, 1 cup cashew nuts, and Craisins®. Stir until well coated. Grease the bottom of each mini baking cup. Drop a heaping teaspoon of cookie into each mini baking cup. Top with one whole cashew per cookie. Cool thoroughly. (See photo on page 58).

Lucky Charms Cookies
Yield: 4 dozen 2½ inch cookies

¾ cup butter, softened
½ cup brown sugar (packed)
¾ cup sugar, divided
2 eggs
1 teaspoon vanilla
2 cups flour
¾ teaspoon baking soda
½ teaspoon salt
2 cups rolled oats
½ cup coconut
½ cup walnuts, chopped
½ cup white chocolate chips
½ cup golden raisins

Lucky Charms Cookies

Preheat oven to 375F. Cream together the butter, brown sugar, ½ cup sugar, eggs and vanilla. Add the flour, baking soda, salt, rolled oats, coconut, walnuts, white chocolate chips and raisins. Stir together until well blended. Roll dough into small balls. Roll into the reserved sugar. Flatten each cookie with the heel of your hand. Bake 12-15 minutes. Cool 1 minute. Remove cookies from baking sheet and place on a cooling rack. (See photo above).

Bridal Shower Horns
Yield: 4 dozen

parchment paper
1 cup butter, softened
¾ cup sugar
2 teaspoons lemon extract
1 cup cottage cheese
½ teaspoon salt
2¼ cups flour

Filling for Bridal Shower Horns

1-12.5 can almond cake
 and pastry filling

Glaze for Bridal Shower Horns
Yield: 4 dozen

1¼ cups powdered sugar
3 tablespoons water
½ teaspoon almond flavoring
¼ teaspoon salt
1 drop pink food coloring

Decorations
⅓ cup sliced almonds
1-1.75 ounce bottle chocolate
 sprinkles
pink and green decorating sugars

The Lemon Poppy Seed Cookies and Mexican Wedding Cake Cookies on the two tiered tray.

Line baking sheets with parchment paper. Preheat oven to 350F. Beat together, butter, sugar, chocolate flavoring, cinnamon, cottage cheese and salt. Fold in flour and mix all ingredients together until smooth. Roll out dough in a shape of a square on floured pastry board or counter top. Cut into 2 inch square pieces. Place a dab of almond cake and pastry filling in the center of each square. Turn each square so it looks like a diamond. Fold center corner of diamond up. Fold each side of the diamond toward the center fold of diamond. It will appear as if it is a small envelope. Roll the dough toward the top of the diamond. Shape into a half moon. Bake for 15 to 20 minutes or until golden brown. Place the powdered sugar in a small bowl. Add the water, almond flavoring, salt and food coloring. Mix all ingredients together until smooth. When the horns are baked, remove from the oven and brush on the glaze. Sprinkle on chocolate sprinkles on half of the horns and almond slices on top of the remaining glazed cookies. Cool horns on a cooling rack. Using this same dough, shape cookies into balls. Place a dab of filling in the center of each ball and roll filling around the ball. Bake at 350F and brush glaze on each ball. Sprinkle with green or pink decorating sugar. (See photo on page 60).

Lemon Poppy Seed Cookies
Yield: 4 dozen 3 inch cookies

parchment paper
1cup butter
1 cup sugar
1 teaspoon lemon extract
½ teaspoon salt
1 cup cottage cheese
2¼ cups flour

Filling for Lemon Poppy Seed Cookies

1-12.5 ounce can poppy seed
cake and pastry filling

Glaze for Lemon Poppy Seed Cookies
Yield: glaze for 4 dozen cookies

1¼ cups powdered sugar
3 tablespoons water
1 teaspoon lemon extract
¼ teaspoon salt

Three tiered cookie tray with Peanut Butter Kisses, Lemon Poppy Seed Cookies, Bridal Shower Horns and Mexican Wedding Cakes.

Line baking sheets with parchment paper. Preheat oven to 350F. Beat together butter, sugar, lemon extract, cinnamon, cottage cheese and salt. Fold in flour and mix all ingredients together until smooth. Roll out dough in a shape of a square on floured pastry board or counter top. Cut into 2 inch square pieces. *Lemon*

Lemon Poppy Seed Cookies, continued

Place a rounded teaspoon poppy seed filling in the center of each square. Fold one end of the square over toward the middle of the filling and the opposite side toward the middle to meet the folded side. Place cookies on baking sheets. Bake for 12-15 minutes or until golden brown. Place powdered sugar in a small bowl. Add water, lemon extract and salt. Whisk all ingredients together until smooth. When cookies are baked, remove from the oven and brush on the glaze. Remove the cookies from the baking sheet and cool on cooling racks. (See photo on page 61).

Tip

There are approximately 40 pretzels per package of 1-8 ounce yogurt and milk chocolate pretzels. There are approximately 400 mints per 12-ounce package.

Bowls of Mixed Nuts, Mints, Yogurt and Chocolate Covered Pretzels
Yield: 30-40 servings

1-8 ounce container yogurt pretzels
1-8 ounce container chocolate covered
  pretzels
1-12 ounce package pastel mints
2-11.5 ounce cans (each) mixed nuts

Divide the yogurt pretzels and chocolate covered pretzels in one divided bowl. Place mints into a candy dish. Place nuts into a small serving dish. (See photo below).

Pretzles and Nuts

Tip
1 gallon lemon lime punch will serve 20 people. Refill punch bowl as needed.

Lemon Lime Punch
Yield: 20 servings

1 gallon lemon lime punch
2 liter bottles white soda
2 ice molds
1 lime, sliced

Lemon Lime Punch
Yield: 40 servings

2 gallons lemon lime punch
4 liter bottles white soda
3 ice molds
2 limes, sliced

Fill ice mold with white soda or water. Freeze until the day of the party. Take ice out of the mold. Place into the punch 10 minutes before serving time. Add the lime slices around the ice mold. (See photo below).

Punch Setup

How to Lay Out the Sweet Table

From Left to Right

1. Lay out a soft pink and striped tablecloth.
2. Swirl a lace tablecloth in an S motion the pink striped tablecloth.
3. Place pearl strings across the front of the pink striped tablecloth.
4. Place one parasol at the very left end of the tablecloth.
5. Place plates after the parasol.
6. Place pink napkins in front of the plates.
7. Place punch cups on the base of the punch bowl.
8. Intersperse one bouquet fresh white tulips between the punch cups.
9. Place punch bowl on the base and fill it with lemon lime punch.
10. Place ice mold in the center of the punch bowl and garnish with lime slices.
11. Next to the punch bowl is a three tiered cookie tray bottom tier with peanut butter kisses, lemon poppy seed cookies and bridal shower horns. The middle tier has Mexican wedding cakes and the top tier has the bridal shower horns shaped into balls and decorated with pink and green sugar.
12. Next to the three tiered tray is the second parasol.
13. In front of the second parasol are the chocolate no-bake cookies in mini foil baking cups.
14. Next to the parasol is the tulip centerpiece.
15. In front of the tulip centerpiece are the peanut butter kisses and peanut butter candy in a crunch shell cookies.
16. The sweetheart cookies are in the back and next to the tulip centerpiece.
17. The lucky charms cookies are next to the peanut butter kisses and peanut butter candy in a crunch shell.

Sweet Table Setup

18. **The romance cookies are next to the lucky charms cookies.**
19. **The lemon poppy seed cookies are on the bottom of the two tiered tray. The remaining Mexican wedding cake cookies are on the top of the tiered tray placed in between the candle holders with tulip candles.**
20. **The mixed nuts are next to the romance cookies.**
21. **The assorted mints are to the right of the mixed nuts and in front of the third parasol.**
22. **The chocolate covered and yogurt covered pretzels are to the left of the mints and nuts.**

Photos from the Drop-By Party

Punch and Cookies Setup

Mints and Nuts

Assorted Cookies

Rachel's Bridal Shower

Main Table

Chicken Croissant Sandwiches
Cucumber Finger Sandwiches
Cheese Wedding Bell
with
Fruit Garnish
Crackers
Raw Vegetables
with
Dill Dip
Deviled Eggs
Strawberries

Dessert Table

Mini Cream Puffs
Mini Éclairs
Mini Cheesecakes
Hello Dolly Bars
Brownies
Sweetheart Bars
Fruit Bowl
with
Rainier & Black Cherries

Chapter 5
Rachel's Bridal Shower

We gave Rachel a shower in mid-July during the warm summer season. We felt that a light and cold buffet would be very appropriate, especially since it was served at 2 p.m. Nine inch glass plates were set out on the buffet. No forks were needed since it was all finger food. The guests enjoyed the buffet. Rachel especially showed her appreciation for giving her a beautiful shower.

Her future mother-in-law and Jason's aunt gave the shower. Since I am the godmother and a caterer, I volunteered to do the food. Betty purchased a beautiful bouquet of fresh flowers for the centerpiece from the local floral designer. She supplied the tablecloth and the beverages.

Since Betty's kitchen and serving area is small, it was a must to keep things simple but attractive for the guests and family. We garnished the food with eye appeal. She made the decaf and regular coffee in the kitchen using two 10-cup coffeepots. She purchased a small see-through plastic tub at the local department store for serving the sodas. She made ice every day for a week to have enough ice.

Aunt Bette and Betty helped make up the cucumber sandwiches. Tiered trays were used to help conserve space for the main menu and dessert teacart. The mini cheesecakes, cream puffs and éclairs were purchased at Sam's Club. Pat made two kinds of bars and arranged two styles of fresh cherries to complete the dessert table. See illustration on page 79.

Betty compiled the games; the guests thoroughly enjoyed the games. Most of the guests stated that they normally don't like to play games at showers, but because Betty presented them in such a creative way, it was great fun.

I stated that women are great talkers and can mingle any time without games. Many of the guests did not know each other upon arrival, but all got along well with each other. Several guests called Betty after the shower and thanked her for a great party. Her neighbor confessed that normally she dreads going to a shower, but this shower was an exceptionally good party.

Low-fat mayonnaise contains 1.5 grams fat and light mayonnaise contains 3.5 grams of fat per quart. Each mini croissant weighs 3/4 ounce (8 to a package).

Tip

I used a small melon scoop to measure out the chicken salad for each sandwich. It is 1½ inches across and holds one tablespoon. The medium-size ice cream scoop is 2 inches across and holds two tablespoons. The large ice cream scoop is 2½ inches across and holds ¼ cup. When serving chicken salad on cocktail size buns, use the medium-size ice cream scoop and the large scoop for the larger buns.

If you do not want to make the chicken salad, purchase it by the pound at the local grocery store. When using cocktail buns, use a little less than two tablespoons of filling per bun. One pound of deli chicken salad makes 14 cocktail sandwiches. One pound of chicken salad makes 16 mini croissant sandwiches.

Chicken Croissant Sandwiches
Yield: 36 mini croissant sandwiches
         (2½ pounds chicken salad)

4-8 ounce boneless, skinless chicken breasts
4 green onions with tops, diced fine
½ cup celery, diced fine
1-8 ounce can crushed pineapple,
   drained
1 tablespoon minced garlic
½ cup red bell pepper, diced
1 teaspoon salt
1 teaspoon pepper
1 teaspoon curry powder
1 cup light mayonnaise
5-6 ounce packages (each) mini croissants
½ cup butter, softened

Chicken Croissant Sandwiches

Cook chicken until no longer pink. Cut chicken into small cubes. Cool thoroughly. Add onions, celery, crushed pineapple, garlic, red bell pepper, salt, pepper and

Chicken Croissant Sandwiches, continued

curry powder. Stir all ingredients together with mayonnaise until well coated. Slice the croissants leaving a hinge. Butter the bottom of each croissant. Place about an ounce of chicken salad on each croissant. Place croissants into the top of a three-tiered tray. (See photo on page 68).

Cucumber Finger Sandwiches
Yield: 40 cucumber sandwiches

Refer to the April Showers chapter on page 6 for the cucumber finger sandwich recipe.

Cheese Wedding Bell with Fruit Garnish
Yield: 20-25 servings

1 pound sharp cheddar cheese spread, softened
1-8 ounce package cream cheese,
  softened
1 teaspoon Worcestershire sauce
¼ teaspoon garlic powder
¼ teaspoon onion powder
½ pound green grapes
½ pound red grapes
1 pint strawberries with hulls

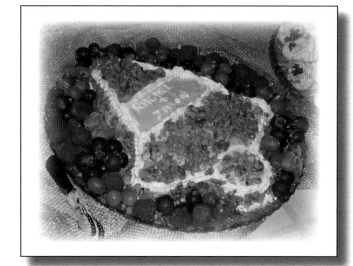

Border for Cheese Wedding Bell

4 ounces cream cheese
½ teaspoon Worcestershire sauce
dash of onion powder

Cheese Wedding Bell with Fruit Garnish

Garnish for Cheese Wedding Bell

½ cup walnuts, finely chopped

Blend cream cheese and cheddar cheese spread. Add Worcestershire sauce, garlic powder and onion powder. Shape cheese mixture into a bell. For the border, beat cream cheese with Worcestershire sauce and onion powder until smooth. Using a pastry bag and a number 28 cake tube, pipe border on the bell. In the middle of

Cheese Wedding Bell with Fruit Garnish, continued

the bell, using a number 4 writing tip, write the bride and groom's name. Sprinkle nuts over top of the bell but not on the writing. Clean and dry the grapes. Cut grapes into 3-4 clumps. Clean and dry the strawberries. Arrange the grapes and strawberries around the wedding bell. Serve with crackers. (See photo on page 69).

Crackers
Yield: 20 servings

1-10 ounce box Wheat Thins®
1-8.5 ounce box Triscuits®

Arrange the crackers in the bottom tray tier or in a basket.

Raw Vegetables
Yield: 12 servings

¾ pound baby carrots
1 pound grape tomatoes
1 pound broccoli flowerets
1 pound cauliflower flowerets
1-12 inch tray or tiered tray

Raw Vegetables
Yield: 20-24 servings

1¼ pounds baby carrots
1½ pounds grape tomatoes
2 pounds broccoli flowerets
2 pounds cauliflower flowerets
1-16 inch tray or tiered tray

Clean and cut the vegetables; arrange on the tiered tray. (See illustration on page 78).

Tip

You can use salad dressing instead of mayonnaise, but I prefer mayonnaise. Salad dressing has a sweeter taste than mayonnaise.

Dill Dip
Yield: 10-12 servings

1-8 ounce container sour cream
1 cup light mayonnaise

Dill Dip
Yield: 20-24 servings

1-16 ounce container sour cream
2 cups light mayonnaise

Dill Dip, Continued

¾ teaspoon Worcestershire sauce	1½ teaspoons Worcestershire sauce
¾ teaspoon lemon juice	1½ teaspoons lemon juice
¼ teaspoon onion salt	½ teaspoon onion salt
¼ teaspoon garlic salt	½ teaspoon garlic salt
½ teaspoon Beau Monde seasoning	1 teaspoon Beau Monde seasoning
3 tablespoons dill weed	5 tablespoons dill weed

In a medium-large bowl, stir sour cream and mayonnaise together. Add Worcestershire, lemon juice, onion salt, garlic salt, Beau Monde seasoning and dill weed. Mix well. Place dill dip into a glass bowl and serve with the raw vegetables. (See illustration on page 78).

Tip
1 large green olive yields 3 slices for the deviled egg garnish. Use 8 large olives to garnish 24 deviled egg halves and 12 large olives to garnish 36 deviled egg halves. Paprika and parsley can be used as the garnish instead of green olives with pimento.

Deviled Eggs
Yield: 12

¼ cup sour cream
2 tablespoons salad dressing

½ teaspoon salt
⅛ teaspoon white pepper
1 teaspoon dry mustard
1 teaspoon lime juice
½ teaspoon minced garlic
3 tablespoons sweet pickle relish
2 drops Tabasco® sauce
½ teaspoon dried dill weed and extra
   dried dill weed for garnishing eggs
8 green olive slices with pimento

Deviled Eggs
Yield: 18

⅓ cup sour cream
¼ cup salad dressing

¾ teaspoon salt
¼ teaspoon white pepper
1½ teaspoons dry mustard
1½ teaspoons lime juice
1 teaspoon minced garlic
¼ cup tablespoons sweet pickle relish
3 drops Tabasco® sauce
1 teaspoon dried dill weed and extra
   dried dill weed for garnishing eggs
12 green olive slices with pimento

Add eggs to an appropriate size pan with cold water. Add salt and lemon juice to the water with eggs. (Refer to page 234). Bring to a boil (5-8 minutes). Shut off the eggs and cover. Let eggs sit in the boiled water for 30 minutes to finish cooking. Peel and cut one egg in half lengthwise to be sure that the yolk is fully cooked.

cooked eggs in cold water. Peel eggs and cut in half lengthwise. Scoop out the yolks and place into a mixing bowl. Place cooked egg white halves on a tray and set aside. Beat egg yolks until they are in fine particles. Add the sour cream and the salad dressing and beat until smooth. Add salt, pepper, dry mustard, lime juice, garlic, sweet pickle relish, Tabasco® sauce and dill weed. Continue to beat the egg yolks until all ingredients are creamy. Insert a 1 E cake tube into a 12 inch pastry bag. (Using a pastry bag gives the deviled eggs a professional touch.) Fill the pastry bag three-quarters full. Fill each reserved egg white half. Garnish with dill weed and an olive slice. (See illustration on page 78).

Mini Cream Puffs
Yield: 70 mini servings

1-30.6 ounce box mini cream puffs

Purchase ready-made mini cream puffs. Arrange the cream puffs in a small glass bowl and place in dish with mini éclairs. (See illustration on page 79).

Mini Éclairs
Yield: 50 mini éclairs

1-25 ounce box mini éclairs

Purchase ready-made mini éclairs. Arrange mini éclairs on a tray with mini cream puffs. (See illustration on page 79).

Tip
One 47.25 ounce box of mini cheesecakes contains 21 New York, 21 white chocolate and 21 chocolate raspberry cheesecakes.

Mini Cheesecakes
Yield: 63 mini cheesecakes

1-47.25 ounce box miniature mini cheesecakes

Arrange the 3 varieties of mini cheesecakes on a tray. (See illustration on page 79).

Hello Dolly Bars
Yield: one 9x9x2-inch pan
      (16 bars)

Crust
½ cup butter, melted (1 stick)
1 cup graham cracker crumbs
Topping
1 cup coconut
1 cup pecans
1 cup semisweet mini chocolate chips
1-14 ounce can sweetened
  condensed milk

Hello Dolly Bars
Yield: one 13x9x2-inch pan
      (30 bars)

Crust
1 cup butter, melted (2 sticks)
2 cups graham cracker crumbs
Topping
2 cups coconut
2 cups pecans
2 cups semisweet mini chocolate chips
2-14 ounce cans (each) sweetened
  condensed milk

Preheat oven to 350F. Melt butter in microwave and pour into pan. Spread graham crackers evenly over melted butter to form a crust. Top with coconut. Top with nuts. Sprinkle chocolate chips over nuts. Pour sweetened condensed milk evenly over the top of chocolate chips. Bake for 25-30 minutes or until golden brown. Cool slightly. Cut into bars. Cover and refrigerate.

Brownies
Yield: 24 ready-made brownies

Purchase 24 brownies from the bakery and arrange on a 3-tiered tray.

Sweetheart Bars
Yield 20 Servings

Refer to Grandma Kay's chapter on page 107 for the sweetheart bars recipe.

Fruit Bowl with Rainier and Black Cherries
Yield: 20 servings

1 pound Rainier cherries
1 pound black cherries
1 bunch fresh parsley, cleaned
Arrange the Rainier and black cherries in a glass-fluted bowl. Garnish with parsley and serve on the dessert table. (See illustration on page 79).

Games

Bride Bingo

B	R	I	D	E
		♥♥♥ Free Space		

Have each guest fill in the squares with what they think the bride's gifts will be. As the gifts are opened, the guests mark off their "item" if they have it on their card. Award prizes for those getting a "bingo."

A Piggy Bank Activity - Winner Takes All

1. Supplies: Spare change, piggy bank, pen, paper, All® detergent
2. Guests add change to the piggy bank.
3. Each person guesses how much change is in the bank by writing it on a piece of paper.
4. Tell everyone that the winner takes all.

What the winner of this game may or may not know is that "All" refers to the laundry detergent and not the piggy bank.

The bride keeps the bank and the money.

This game is a fun and easy activity to get the couple's bank account started.

The mother of the bride-to-be won the All® detergent. It was great fun to watch the expressions of each guest's face.

The Unusual Bridal Shower Game

This is an unusual game;
It really claims no fame.

It is a game that is fun to play;
With guests on the bridal shower day.

So please give me your attention;
And listen up to what is mentioned.

In the end, whoever scores the most;
Will receive a prize and a toast.

Now, since you are fashionable ladies
Give yourself 5 if you are wearing shades.

Give yourself 5 if you are wearing red;
6 more with a hat on your head.

By now you are hoping to win;
Take away 2 with a tan on your skin.

Give yourself 6 if your garment is tight;
Add 1 if your lipstick is on right.

Add 5 more if your shoes are white;
And take away 3 if your top is too bright.

Now count all your buttons, for each you get two;
And take away 1 for each button that's blue.

Give yourself 5 if your neckline is high;
And why not take 10 for blue in your eye.

10 more points for a flower on your clothes;
Take away 5 if you forgot to wear hose.

If your husband you kissed today – add 9;
If you didn't, subtract 12 – you're subject to fine.

This is the end…there isn't anymore;
Who is the lucky lady with the highest score?

After the gifts were opened and games were played, the story of how Jason and Rachel met began to unfold.

Rachel's Story on How She and Jason Met

Rachel said that while she was attending college she worked in a pizza parlor near the campus. One evening, Jason and his friend Craig came into the restaurant, and she thought Jason was sweet as she waited on them. A few weeks later when Jason came back, Rachel asked him out for a drink after her shift was done. Jason agreed and this led to the couple's first date. They liked each other immediately and learned they had a lot in common. That evening was the start of a wonderful relationship and romance that led to marriage. At the shower, Rachel confessed that after two months of dating, she told her family that she was going to marry this man. Everyone smiled at her as she told her story.

Jason's Wedding Proposal

Jason wanted the proposal to be creative and a big surprise. He purchased a remote controlled Wall-E robot from eBay that was a replica of the Pixar film character. Shortly before Christmas, Jason called Rachel to meet him at the theater where he worked as a stagehand. When Rachel arrived, the theater was empty and as she approached the stage, Wall-E rolled to mid-stage with a ring box between his arms. "Will you marry me?" Jason shouted from the light booth. Rachel shouted enthusiastically towards the back of the theater, "Yes!" Rachel put the ring on her finger, a diamond that originally belonged to Jason's great grandmother. After the proposal, the couple met Rachel's family for dinner, where she regaled the story of the proposal.

The Buffet Layout with the Cold Appetizer Table

Gold yellow was the predominate color used for the shower.
1. Cover the table with a gold yellow tablecloth and gold lace overlay.
2. Cover the teacart with a yellow tablecloth and a white lace overlay.
3. Place glass plates and napkins on the table. (no silverware needed)
4. Arrange food from left to right-cucumber finger sandwiches, cheese wedding bell, salt and pepper and 2 trays of deviled eggs.
5. In the back left corner is a tiered tray with chicken croissant sandwiches the top tray, assorted raw vegetables in the middle tray. The Triscuit® and Wheat Thins® are in the bottom tray.
6. The dill dip is to the right of the raw vegetables and crackers.
7. The fresh bouquet of flowers is in the center of the table.

Main Buffet Appetizer Setup

The Buffet Layout on the Teacart with Finger Desserts

1. **Starting right to left--one large tier tray with desserts**
   Top tier – éclairs
   Middle tier – brownies with yellow jimmies and hello dolly bars
   Bottom tier – outer layer with hello dolly bars
   Middle layer with sweetheart bars
   Inner layer with brownies with yellow jimmies
2. **The teddy bear bride and groom is the centerpiece.**
3. **Black cherries around the outside of the bowl with Rainier cherries**
   in the center of the bowl with a parsley garnish around the black cherries
4. **Mini cream puffs in a bowl with mini éclairs on the tray with cream puffs**
5. **Napkins**

Dessert Buffet Setup

Chapter 6
Grandma Kay's Garden Bridal Shower
Grandpa Ray's Bachelor Party

Grandma Kay's Garden Bridal Shower Introduction

Grandma Kay fell in love with her high school sweetheart. Her father forbade her to marry him and insisted that she marry the farm boy next door. She put up a fuss for a long time, but eventually gave in and married her neighbor. She heard through the grapevine that her sweetheart found someone else while serving his country and had moved away to California. At their 50th class reunion Grandma Kay was shocked to see her old fling, Ray. Both had lost their spouses about the same time. They spent the whole evening together catching up. Ray told Grandma that she was just as beautiful as years ago. He promised her he would write and call often. He kept his word. Before the year was over, he proposed to her. He was willing to move to Kansas since she was so close to her family. Grandma Kay loved to garden, growing the finest flowers and vegetables. She grew beautiful iris flowers and the most luscious Big Boy tomatoes, many herbs and a multitude of other vegetables. She also had many apple trees in her yard. She made countless apple pies and canned hundreds of jars of applesauce. She enjoyed many community events. Grandma Kay had a heart of gold and volunteered for many charities.

Her granddaughters and great granddaughters planned and prepared a fabulous garden bridal shower for Grandma Kay. The family flew Ray into Kansas the night before the shower to surprise her. The entire family wanted to meet him. Ray was received with open arms. They were delighted to become acquainted with their future step Grandpa Ray. They all felt he was a delight and great for Grandma Kay.

About an hour before the shower, Grandma Kay and Ray walked through the apple orchard. He presented her with a beautiful engagement ring. Grandma Kay was aglow and her face radiated with much pleasure as she showed off her new diamond at the shower.

The granddaughters also made Grandma Kay a picture board with photos from Grandma Kay's life. Each guest tried to guess Grandma Kay's age in the pictures. The person with the most correct answers won a prize.

The shower was a great success. Afterwards, the family placed all the pictures from the shower into a scrapbook photo album and gave it to Grandma Kay.

Grandma Kay's Photo

A Tribute to Grandma Kay

Today is your special day,
Hoping everything comes your way.

Enjoy your family, guests and day,
With shower cards, gifts and play.

A mother, a grandmother, a friend,
True blue to mankind to the very end.

A talented lady and very smart,
Always there, with a loving heart.

Beautiful with wit and charm,
Full of wisdom and never harm.

May this sincere tribute sent by a dove,
Represent caring thoughts and all our love.

Best wishes upon your upcoming wedding day,
Along with presents of happy memories to be with you always.

Tip

I like to greet the guests with one hot and one cold appetizer. Serve punch or a favorite beverage with the appetizers for starters and for a great ice breaker.

What Is a Crab Cake?

A crab cake is an American dish made of crabmeat along with other ingredients such as bread crumbs, milk, eggs, onions and seasonings. Sometimes red and green bell peppers are also added.

Two styles of crab cakes are Maryland and Boardwalk crab cakes. Maryland crab cakes are fried or broiled. Boardwalk crab cakes are filled with stuffing, breaded, deep fried and served on hamburger buns. Various kinds of crabmeat can be used when making crab cakes. Blue crab is from the Chesapeake Bay area and is very traditional.

Crab cakes are popular along the coasts of the Mid-Atlantic States, Northern California and the Gulf states. Basically, crab cakes are popular wherever the crab industry thrives. Crab cakes vary in size from small to large, served as a sandwich on a hamburger bun. Tartar sauce, Remoulade or even ketchup is served with crab cakes.

In the Pacific Northwest and Northern California, Dungeness crab is a popular ingredient for crab cakes. Dungeness crab flesh has a delicate flavor. It is sweeter than the flesh of other crabs.

What is a Remoulade Sauce?

Remoulade Sauce originated in France. It is made with mayonnaise, minced capers, chives, fresh parsley and white pepper. Some recipes also call for minced anchovies.

What is Tartar Sauce?

Tartar sauce is spelled tartare sauce in Europe. Tartar Sauce is made with a mayonnaise base and chopped dill or sweet pickle relish and Worcestershire sauce. I like to add a little horseradish to the tartar sauce.

What is Lime Sauce?

Lime Sauce is made with mayonnaise, sour cream, lime juice, lime peel, dehydrated onion, white pepper and Tabasco® sauce . This is my favorite sauce to serve with the crab cakes.

Tip

The crab appetizer recipe can be doubled and still be tasty. Usually I plan on serving two crab cake appetizers per person. The crab cakes can be made a day ahead of time and heated on the day of the party. Seven dozen crackers are in one 8-ounce box of Triscuits®. One 8-ounce container of Weight Watchers® reduced fat whipped cream cheese frosts 7 dozen Triscuits®. Use one teaspoon of cool lime sauce on top of each crab cake. There are 12 tablespoons in ¾ cup or 36 teaspoons. I like to use freshly squeezed lime juice in the cool lime sauce.

Crab Cake Appetizers
Yield: 30-34 mini crab cakes

4-6 ounce cans (each) crabmeat
2 tablespoons butter, divided
4 tablespoons olive oil, divided
⅓ cup green bell pepper, diced
⅓ cup red bell pepper, diced
⅓ cup celery, diced
⅓ cup minced onion
½ teaspoon minced garlic
½ cup dried Italian bread crumbs
½ teaspoon ground pepper
1 teaspoon Old Bay® seasoning
1 teaspoon dry mustard

2 tablespoons minced fresh parsley
1 egg
¼ cup mayonnaise
2 teaspoon Worcestershire sauce
½ teaspoon ground pepper
2 teaspoons fresh lemon juice
¼ teaspoon Tabasco® sauce
Parchment paper
1 cup Panko® bread crumbs
1-8 ounce container
  Weight Watchers® reduced
  fat whipped cream cheese spread
1-8 ounce box Triscuit® crackers

Drain the crabmeat and set aside. Sauté red and green bell peppers, celery, onion and garlic in one tablespoon of butter and 2 tablespoons oil for about 3-4 minutes or until tender. Drain and dab vegetables with paper towel. Cool slightly. In a large bowl, mix together crabmeat, Italian bread crumbs, Old Bay® seasoning, dry mustard, scallions, parsley and egg. Mix in sautéed vegetables/garlic mixture. In a small bowl, whisk together mayonnaise, Worcestershire sauce, pepper, lemon juice and Tabasco® sauce. Add this mixture to the breadcrumb mixture. Gently mix the crab mixture by hand until combined. Line the cookie sheet with parchment paper. Using a tablespoon scoop, form the crab cakes into small balls. Roll the crab cake balls into the Panko® bread crumbs. Flatten them into 1½ inch round crab cakes. Place on the cookie sheet. Cover with plastic wrap and refrigerate for at least one hour. In a large skillet, add 1 tablespoon butter and 2 tablespoons olive oil. Place crab cakes into the heated skillet. Cook on both sides until golden brown. Drain crab cakes on a paper towel. Lightly frost the Triscuit® crackers with cream cheese. Top each Triscuit® with a crab cake. Place 12-15 crab cake cake appetizers onto a microwave dish. Microwave for 15-20 seconds to slightly heat. Place crab cake appetizers on a serving plate lined with a doily. Place a dab of cool lime sauce in the center of each crab cake and butler-pass these appetizers or set them out on the buffet with a dish of cool lime sauce and guests can help themselves.

Cool Lime Sauce
Yield: ¾ cup

½ cup light mayonnaise
¼ cup sour cream
1 tablespoon lime juice
2 teaspoons grated lime peel
1 teaspoon Worcestershire sauce
1 teaspoon dehydrated onion
¼ teaspoon white pepper
2 drops Tabasco® Sauce

Cool Lime Sauce
Yield: 1½ cups

1 cup light mayonnaise
½ cup sour cream
2 tablespoons limejuice
3 teaspoons lime peel
2 teaspoons Worcestershire sauce
2 teaspoons dehydrated onion
½ teaspoon white pepper
3 drops Tabasco® sauce

Tip
Allowing three per person, seventy two ham roll-ups serve 24 guests. Some guests do not like olives and may pass on this particular appetizer.

Ham Roll-Ups
Yield: 72 ham roll-ups
       (24 servings)

12-4x6 slices ham, sliced thin
12-ounces cream cheese, divided
1-15 ounce jar green olives
   stuffed with pimientos, drained
   and dried (72 olives)
¾ teaspoon Worcestershire sauce
¾ teaspoon onion powder

Lay ham slices out in a line on paper towel. Dab the ham with paper towel to dry off the excess moisture. Soften the cream cheese. Beat cream cheese until smooth. Add the Worcestershire sauce and onion powder. Beat until creamy. Evenly divide cream cheese mixture and spread over the entire surface of each slice of ham. Line up 6 olives in a row at the short end of each ham slice with the pimento centers facing the same direction. Starting at the end with olives, tightly roll-up into a cylinder. Place ham roll-ups on a plate. Cover with plastic wrap and chill for at least 3 hours or overnight. Slice each ham roll into 6 pieces, exposing one olive per spiral.

Tip

Whenever I serve the mini turkey croissant sandwiches, I make them up ahead of time on the day of the party. I slice each croissant and make a hinge. I butter the bottom of each croissant and place a slice of rolled up turkey onto each croissant. Close the top of the croissant to form the sandwich. Tomatoes, lettuce and mayonnaise are served on the side at the buffet line next to the sandwiches. Figure one and half sandwiches per person. Some will take two sandwiches and others will pass when there is a variety of foods. The grocery store sells croissants 10-12 per box. Mini croissants can also be purchased in large quantities from 36-48 per box..

Chart for Mini Turkey Croissant Sandwiches

Number of guests	Number of croissants to purchase
10	15
20	30
30	45
40	55
50	65

Turkey Croissant Sandwiches

Tip

For a smaller group, purchase a pint of mayonnaise. For a larger group, purchase a quart of mayonnaise. For any size group, serve the mayonnaise in a small bowl. It is better to refill the mayonnaise bowl than to let it set out for a long length of time. The extra mayonnaise in the jar should be refrigerated and used as needed another time.

Usually a half of a head of lettuce is plenty for a smaller crowd and a large head of lettuce serves 50 sandwiches. Break the core of the lettuce by pounding the head down on the counter top. Pull out the core. Run cold water in the core area and rinse the head lettuce well. Tear lettuce into small pieces to fit the mini croissant sandwiches. Dab the lettuce dry and place the lettuce onto a serving tray.

I like to use Roma tomatoes. One Roma tomato yields 6 slices. I usually figure 8-10 extra slices of tomatoes per number of sandwiches.

Chart for Tomato Slices

Number of sandwiches sandwiches	Number of Tomato Slices	Number of Tomatoes
15	24	4
20	30	5
30	42	7
40	48	8
50	60	10

Tip

Omit the white pepper and chili powder when making a milder tomato basil soup. The tomato basil soup freezes well. Place leftover soup into individual containers and freeze. Using an aspic heart cutter, cut out several hearts from a red bell pepper for a garnish and reserve chopped scallion tops for a garnish. A garnish of parsley, sour cream and red bell pepper heart is an excellent garnish for the tomato basil soup.

Tomato Basil Soup
Yield: 6 servings

½ cup vegetable broth
1 cup mild picante sauce
1-14 ounce can diced
  chili tomatoes
1 tablespoons minced garlic
⅓ cup leek, chopped
½ cup scallions without tops, chopped
1-ounce fresh basil leaves, whole
1 teaspoons cumin
⅛ teaspoon white pepper
¼ teaspoon chili powder
1-15 ounce can Southwest style
  crispy corn, drained
1-15 ounce can black beans,
  drained and rinsed
1-15 ounce can vegetable broth

Tomato Basil Soup
Yield: 15 servings

1 cup vegetable broth
3 cups mild picante sauce
2-14 ounce cans (each) diced
  chili tomatoes
2 tablespoons minced garlic
½ cup leek, chopped
¾ cups scallions without tops, chopped
2½ ounces fresh basil leaves, whole
2 ¼ teaspoons cumin
¼ teaspoon white pepper
½ teaspoon chili powder
2-15 ounce cans (each) Southwest style
  crispy corn, drained
2-15 ounce cans (each) black beans,
  drained and rinsed
2-15 ounce cans (each) vegetable broth

Tip
Larger batches of soup ingredients will have to be divided due to the size of the blender. Divide the picante sauce, tomatoes, garlic, leek, scallions and fresh basil into four batches when making 30 servings and into five batches for 50 servings. For larger groups it is wise to set out bowls of garnishes and let the guests help themselves unless servers are at hand to help serve the guests. A 16-ounce container of sour cream is enough to serve 25 people, for not everyone will take sour cream.

(Vegetable broth is sold in 14.5 ounce cans at your local grocery store).

Tomato Basil Soup
Yield: 30 servings

1½ cups vegetable broth
7 cups mild picante sauce
4-14 cans (each) plus 1 cup diced
  chili tomatoes
3 tablespoons minced garlic
6 tablespoons leek

Tomato Basil Soup
Yield: 50 servings

2 cup vegetable broth
10 cups mild picante sauce
6-14 ounce cans (each) diced
  chili tomatoes
¼ cup minced garlic
½ cup leek

Tomato Basil Soup, continued

¾ cup scallions without tops, chopped
3 ounces fresh basil leaves, whole
3 teaspoons cumin
1 teaspoon chili powder
½ teaspoon white pepper
3-15 ounce cans (each) Southwest style crispy corn, drained and rinsed
3-15 ounce cans (each) black beans, drained and rinsed
3-15 ounce cans (each) vegetable broth

1 cup scallions without tops, chopped
4 ounces fresh basil leaves, whole
4 teaspoons cumin
1½ teaspoons chili powder
1 teaspoon white pepper
5-15 ounce cans (each) Southwest style crispy corn, drained and rinsed
5-15 ounce cans (each) black beans, drained and rinsed
4-15 ounce cans (each) vegetable broth

In a blender, place picante sauce, tomatoes, garlic, leek, scallions and fresh basil. Blend ingredients on high for about 10 seconds. In a medium stockpot, stir vegetable broth into the blended ingredients. Add cumin, white pepper, chili powder, corn and black beans. Stir all ingredients together until well blended. Simmer over low heat for 25-30 minutes or until the soup is heated through. Garnish each bowl of soup with a sprig of parsley or a dab of sour cream and 1½ teaspoons of chopped scallion tops; place a red bell pepper heart in the center of the parsley or sour cream. Enjoy!

Tip

I received rave reviews on the garden brunch bake at the bridal shower. Make this dish one day ahead of time and warm it up on the day of the party. A microwave will not work to re-warm this recipe. The microwave method softens the puff pastry and can make this dish soggy. (Method I) On the day of the shower, preheat the oven to 300F and bake the brunch bake, whole, 20 to 30 minutes or until thoroughly heated. (Method II) Preheat the oven to 275F. Slice the garden brunch bake into 20 slices and place slices on a lightly greased cookie sheet. Bake for 10-20 minutes or until thoroughly heated. Transfer the brunch bake pieces onto a large serving tray. Serve the brunch bake with the celebration salad and assorted breads. See recipes on page 96-98 and 102-106.

To make 40 servings of brunch bake, use two separate bowls to make the egg filling for each of the 20 servings. Line two separate spring-form pans with puff pastry; assemble each brunch bake in the recommended steps from the brunch bake recipe for best results. See illustration on page 82 and line drwing on page 96-97.

You can make and bake the garden brunch bake at 375 F for 55-60 minutes on the day of the party. Place the baked brunch bake on a platter and garnish it with red bell pepper and tomato slices. Slice the brunch bake to order as guests go through the buffet line.

Garden Brunch Bake
Yield: 20 servings

2-1 pound boxes (each)
 puff pastry sheets
1-10 ounce package
 frozen spinach, thawed and
 squeezed dry
1-15 ounce container ricotta cheese
1 bunch scallions, chopped
⅓ cup leek, chopped
2 teaspoons minced garlic
2-8 ounce packages (each)
 Neufchatel cheese, softened
12 eggs, beaten
2 teaspoons dried basil
2 teaspoons dried oregano
1 teaspoon white pepper
1 cup red bell pepper, chopped
1 cup green bell pepper, chopped
1 cup celery, chopped
2 cups mushrooms, sliced
2 cups Mexican style four cheese blend
 (cheddar, Asadero, Quesoquesalla
 and Monterey Jack Cheese), divided
no-stick baking spray

Egg Wash for Garden Brunch Bake

1 egg
1 teaspoon milk

Garden Brunch Bake Serving Suggestions Illustrations

Preheat oven to 375F. Spray a 10-inch spring-form pan with no-stick baking spray. Roll out three puff pastry sheets 10x10 inches. Place 1 sheet to cover bottom of the pan. Cut the second pastry sheet into 2 or 3 pieces to fit the sides of the pan making sure that the crust covers the entire pan tightly and all seams are pressed together (fig.1). Mix together the spinach, ricotta cheese, scallions, leek and garlic. Place half of the spinach mixture on the bottom of the puff pastry lined pan (fig.2). Sprinkle with red and green bell peppers. Top with 1 cup Mexican cheese. Beat the Neufchatel cheese. Add the beaten eggs, basil, oregano, and white pepper; stir until mixture is blended well. Pour over the Mexican cheese layer. Repeat next layer with remaining spinach mixture. Top with celery and mushrooms. Sprinkle remaining cheese over layer (fig.3). Cover the brunch bake with one puff pastry sheet to form the top of the brunch bake. Seal the edges of the pastry (fig.4). Beat the egg and milk together to make the egg wash. Brush the egg wash over the top of the puff pastry (fig.5). Place slits at random on the top of the puff pastry to let out the steam. Cut out puff pastry hearts with an aspic cutter and place them in a circle-like fashion. Bake for 50-60 minutes or until puff pastry is golden brown and toothpick inserted in the center comes out clean. The eggs in the brunch bake should be firm and the puff pastry should be golden brown.

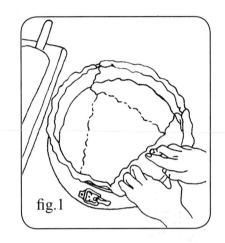

fig.1

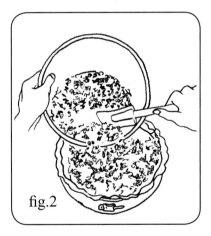

fig.2

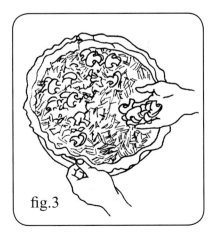

fig.3

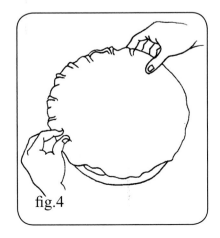

fig.4

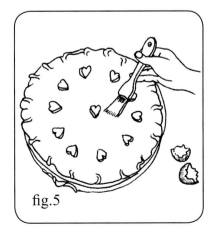

fig.5

Tip

One pound of celebration salad feeds four people. For larger quantities buy 4 pound bags of cole slaw mix from Sam's Club or a local wholesale dealer. Grocery stores sell coleslaw mix in 14-ounce bags.

A food processor is helpful for shredding red or green cabbage. When making 50 servings, buy a 16 ounce can of crushed pineapple. This size can yield approximately half pineapple with the remainder in juice. I like to use honey crisp apples in the celebration salad. However, honey crisp apples are often seasonal. A pink lady apple is sweet and tastes much like the honey crisp apple. I use a red delicious apple when making the bird of paradise for a showy garnish. There is 1 cup of water chestnuts to an 8 ounce can. Prepare and mix all the salad ingredients together one day ahead of time. Mix the dressing together in a separate bowl and store in the refrigerator overnight. Mix the dressing into the salad on the day of the party. Garnish the salad with the bird of paradise and apple wedges. Keep salad in the refrigerator until serving time.

While portions of ingredients are listed, a person can add a little more of this or that (ingredient-wise) as long as the green cabbage and dressing portions are consistent.

Celebration Salad
Yield: 12 servings

2 pounds shredded green cabbage
  (8 cups)
1 cup shredded red cabbage
¾ cup golden figs, chopped
1 cup dates, cut into circles
1 pink lady apple, cored and diced
1-8 ounce can crushed pineapple,
  drained
1 tablespoon minced garlic
1 tablespoon scallions, sliced
1½ cups celery, diced
2/3 cup sliced water chestnuts,
  drained and julienned
1 tablespoon toasted sesame seeds
3 tablespoons sliced honey
  roasted almonds

Celebration Salad
Yield: 25 servings

5 pounds shredded green cabbage
  (20 cups)
2 cups shredded red cabbage
1 cup golden figs, chopped
1¼ cup dates, cut into circles
2 pink lady apples, cored and diced
1-16 ounce can crushed pineapple,
  drained
1½ tablespoons minced garlic
2 tablespoons scallions, sliced
2 cups celery, diced
1-8 ounce can sliced water chestnuts,
  drained and julienned
2 tablespoons toasted sesame seeds
1-3.5 ounce package sliced honey
  roasted almonds

Celebration Salad
Yield: 50 servings

8 pounds shredded green cabbage
  (32 cups)
3 cups shredded red
  cabbage
1½ cups golden figs, chopped
1½ cup dates, cut into circles
3 pink lady apples,
  cored and diced
1-16 ounce can crushed
  pineapple, drained
5 teaspoons minced garlic
3 tablespoons scallions, sliced with tops
2¼ cups celery, diced
3 tablespoons toasted sesame seeds
2-3.5 packages (each) sliced honey
  roasted almonds

Chart for Orange Ginger Vinaigrette Dressing

Yield: 12 servings	Yield: 25 servings	Yield: 50 servings
1 cup sour cream	2 cups sour cream	4 cups sour cream
1 cup bottled orange ginger vinaigrette dressing	2 cups bottled orange ginger vinaigrette dressing	4 cups bottled orange ginger vinaigrette dressing
1 teaspoon white pepper	1½ teaspoon white pepper	1¾ teaspoon white pepper

In a bowl mix together the green and red cabbage. Add the figs, dates, apples, pineapple, garlic, scallions, celery, water chestnuts, sesame seeds and almonds. Add the pepper to the salad dressing and sour cream. Combine the orange ginger vinaigrette dressing, sour cream and pepper. Whisk together until smooth and creamy. Stir dressing into the salad and toss until well coated. Place salad into a glass fluted bowl. Follow directions on page 100 for making the bird of paradise. Core and quarter an extra apple into 7-3 inch by ¾ inch thick wedges. Place the bird of paradise in the center of the bowl and stand up the wedges into each fluted edge. Refrigerate until serving time. (See illustrations on page 101).

Chart for the Number of Bird of Paradise Garnishes Per Yield

Yield: 12 servings	Yield: 25 servings	Yield: 50 servings
1 bird of paradise	2 bird of paradise	3 bird of paradise

Bird of Paradise

Yield: one bird of paradise
per 12 servings
2 large red delicious apples
(reserve one apple for
decoration)

Using a sharp paring knife, slice off a little less than one third of the side of the apple to create a flat surface (fig.1). Set the slice aside and save, as it will be carved into the neck and the head of the bird. Place the apple so it rests on its flat surface with the stem end facing you. Using a small sharp paring knife, cut a small V shaped wedge from the top of the apple. Set this V-wedge aside and cut another V-wedge just a little larger than the first one (fig.2). Continue cutting V-wedges (each a little larger than the preceding one) until you have five or six (fig.3). If a piece breaks off, do not worry because the sections will hold together when assembled. After cutting the top wedges to form the fan of feathers, turn the apple on its side and cut one large wedge for a wing. Repeat on the opposite side. Place the apple again on its flat surface with stem side facing you. Take the largest of the graduated V-wedges and place it in the top cut out of the apple (fig.4). Extend the wedge so that it protrudes slightly less than halfway beyond the back of the apple. Layer the next size smaller V-wedge on and extend it out to the rear of the first already placed V-wedge. Continue until all the graduated V-wedges are used and a feather fan has been created down the top center of the bird (fig.5). Place a side V-wedge into its corresponding cut out. Extend it back beyond the body of the bird to create the wing. Repeat with the other side. Take reserved slice and carve out a long curved neck with attached head. Insert a toothpick into the body on an angle and attach the neck with head (fig.6). Prevent darkening by squeezing lemon juice over the entire surface of the bird.

Cut the second delicious apple into 7 wedges, each 3 inches long by ¾ inch thick Squeeze lemon juice over the pieces to prevent darkening. These will be used around the perimeter of the top of the salad. (See the diagram and illustration on page 101).

Step by Step Illustrations (fig. 1-6)

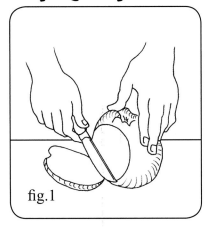

fig.1

Slice off a little less than one third of the side of the apple to create a flat surface.

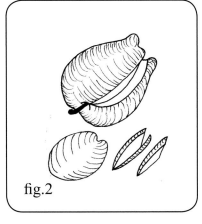

fig.2

Cut graduated V-wedges on the top of the apple.

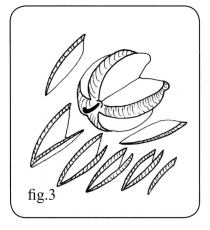

fig.3

Cut graduated V-wedge on each side of the apple.

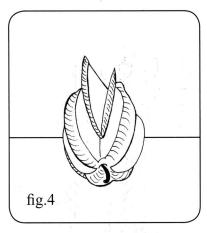

fig.4

Place V-wedge in the center of the apple.

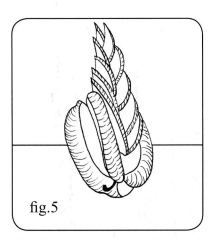

fig.5

Continue to place graduated V-wedges to form feathers down the center.

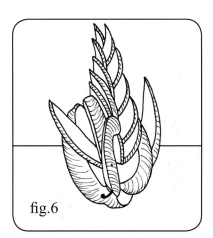

fig.6

Complete the feathers for the sides. Take reserved slice and carve out a long curved neck with attached head. Attach the neck with head to the body of the bird.

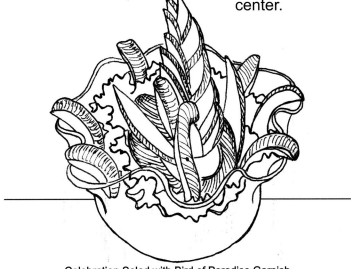

Celebration Salad with Bird of Paradise Garnish

See extra details on how to make the bird of paradise on page 100.

The grandchildren thought it was a good idea to surprise Grandma Kay and make bread for her shower. In fact, they also wanted to make extra loaves of bread for door prizes for the guests. Every time Grandma Kay had company for dinner, she sent home an extra loaf of bread with several of her guests. She didn't have a clue that her grandchildren knew how to make most of Grandma Kay's favorite breads. They were very excited about their special surprise.

General Information on Yeast Breads

1. Yeast breads require pans lightly greased with shortening or no-stick baking spray.
2. Once yeast breads are baked, remove from the pans immediately.
3. Scald milk to destroy enzymes. Dry milk does not need to be scalded.
4. A temperature of 130F kills yeast.
5. In bread making, ½ cake or one envelope of dry yeast is used to one cup of liquid for a 4-5 hour preparation period.
6. For best results, use 95F lukewarm water for compressed yeast and 105 or warm water for active dry yeast. Do not use hot water. Too much heat kills the yeast and not enough heat retards its action.
7. Lightly grease the top of the bread dough during the rising times to prevent formation of a crust.

Tip

All the breads can be made up and frozen one week ahead of the party time.

Grandma Kay's Cinnamon Casserole Bread
Yield: 1-10 inch bread in round casserole dish

3 cups bread flour
1-¼ ounce package active dry yeast
1 egg, at room temperature
1 teaspoon cinnamon
1¼ cups evaporated milk
3 tablespoons sugar
2 tablespoons unsalted butter
1 teaspoon salt
1 tablespoon cinnamon-sugar
no-stick baking spray

Grandma Kay's Cinnamon Casserole Bread, continued

In a five-quart mixer bowl, mix together flour, yeast and cinnamon with dough hook. Add the egg and beat for two minutes. In a saucepan, combine the milk, sugar, butter and salt. Heat over low heat, stirring constantly until butter melts and milk is warm. Remove from the heat. Slowly add the milk and butter mixture to the flour and yeast mixture. With the dough hook, continue to beat the bread ingredients for three to four more minutes. Scrape sides as needed. Place dough into a greased stainless steel or glass bowl. Lightly grease the top of the bread with no-stick baking spray. Cover with plastic wrap and a towel. Let the bread rise in a warm area draft-free place until dough doubles in size. Punch down and knead by hand for about 4 minutes. Return the bread to the lightly greased casserole dish and evenly spread the bread into the 10 inch round casserole dish. Sprinkle the top of the bread with the cinnamon-sugar mixture. Set aside on top of the range. Cover with plastic wrap and a towel. Let the dough rise again until double in size. Bake at 350F for 45-50 minutes or until toothpick inserted in center of bread comes out clean. Place on a cooling rack and let stand for about 5 minutes. Remove the bread from the casserole dish. Cool thoroughly for about one hour. Place bread into a 1 gallon size plastic bag and store in the freezer until a day before the party.

Grandma Kay's Craisin® and Nut Bread
Yield: one 10 inch heart shaped pan

1½ cups whole wheat flour
1½ cups white bread flour
1-¼ ounce package dry yeast
1 egg, at room temperature
1¼ cups evaporated milk
1 teaspoon cinnamon
1 teaspoon salt
3 tablespoons sugar
1 tablespoon honey
2 tablespoons butter
½ cup pecans, chopped
½ cup Craisins®
no-stick baking spray
1 tablespoon cinnamon-sugar mixture

In a 5 quart mixing bowl place flours and the dry yeast. Using a dough hook, beat together for 1 minute. Add the egg and beat for another minute, scraping the sides of the bowl as needed. In a saucepan, combine the milk, cinnamon, salt, sugar, honey and butter, stirring constantly over low heat until butter is melted and milk is warmed. Remove from the heat and cool slightly to room temperature. Slowly add the mixture to the yeast/flour and egg mixture. Beat for 3 minutes. Stir in the pecans and Craisins®. Lightly grease bowl with no-stick cooking spray. Place bread into bowl. Lightly grease the top of the bread with no-stick cooking spray. Cover with plastic wrap and a towel. Set on top of the stove or a warm area. Let the bread rise until double in size. Punch down the dough. Place onto a lightly floured countertop and knead for 3 minutes. Spray no-stick baking spray into a heart shaped pan and evenly spread the dough. Lightly grease the top of the bread with no-stick baking spray. Cover with plastic wrap and a towel in an area away from draft and let rise again until double in size. Sprinkle the top of bread with cinnamon-sugar mixture. Bake at 350 F for 35-45 minutes or until toothpick inserted in the center of the bread comes out clean. Remove the bread from the pan. Store in a one-gallon plastic bag and freeze until one day before the party.

Tip

Grandma Kay always used baked potatoes when making the dill bread. She said, "boiled potatoes hold too much liquid and would spoil the bread." You can also use instant mash potatoes. I use the original ready-made mashed potatoes and white bread flour for best results.

Potato Dill Bread
Yield: one 9 inch loaf pan

3 cups white bread flour
1-¼ ounce package dry yeast
1 egg, at room temperature
½ cup cold mashed potatoes
1 cup evaporated milk
1 tablespoon dried dill weed
1 tablespoon dehydrated onion
1 teaspoon salt
¼ cup sugar
2 tablespoons butter
no-stick baking spray

Potato Dill Bread, continued

In a 5 quart mixing bowl, add flour and the yeast. With a dough hook, beat for one minute. Add the egg and beat for another minute. Add the potatoes and beat another minute. In a saucepan, over low heat, combine the milk, dill weed, onion, salt, sugar and butter. Stir mixture constantly until the butter is melted. Remove from the heat and cool slightly. Add the liquid ingredients to the flour mixture. Beat with a dough hook for four minutes. Place bread in a lightly greased medium size glass or stainless steel bowl with no-stick cooking spray. Lightly grease the top of the bread with no-stick baking spray. Cover with plastic wrap and a towel. Place out of a draft or in a warm area. Let rise until double in size. Punch down the bread. On a lightly floured countertop, knead the bread for four minutes or until dough is no longer sticky. Roll out dough medium thickness. Roll the dough up like a diploma to hide the seams. Place the seam side down into a lightly greased loaf pan with no stick baking spray. Grease the top of the bread with no-stick baking spray. Cover with plastic wrap and a towel. Let rise again until double in size. Remove the plastic wrap and towel. Bake at 350F for 35-45 minutes or until toothpick inserted in the center comes out clean. Remove from the pan and cool on cooling rack. Store in the freezer in a one gallon freezer bag until one day before the party.

Grandma Kay's Hearty Whole Wheat Bread
Yield: 10 inch bread in a casserole dish

3 cups whole wheat flour
1-¼ ounce package dry yeast
1 egg, at room temperature
1¼ cups evaporated milk
2 tablespoons sugar
1 tablespoon honey
1 teaspoon salt
2 tablespoons butter
no-stick baking spray
shortening

In a 5 quart mixing bowl, place flour and the dry yeast. With the dough hook, beat together for one minute. Add the egg and beat for another minute. In a medium size saucepan, over low heat, add milk, sugar, honey, salt and butter, stirring constantly until the butter is melted. Remove from the heat and cool slightly. Add the milk mixture to the flour and yeast mixture. Continue to knead the bread with a dough hook for 3 more minutes. Spray medium size glass or stainless steel bowl with no-stick baking spray. Place bread dough into the bowl. Spray the top of the bread with no-stick baking spray. Cover with plastic wrap and a towel. On top of the stove or in a warm area, let the dough rise until double in size. Punch down. Place the dough onto a lightly floured board and knead by hand for 3 minutes. Lightly grease casserole bowl or loaf pan with no-stick spray. Place dough into the bowl or loaf pan. Lightly grease the top of the bread with no-stick baking spray. Cover with plastic wrap and a towel and let it rise until double in size. Remove towel and plastic wrap; bake at 350F for 35-45 minutes or until toothpick inserted in the center comes out clean. Remove the bread from the casserole dish or loaf pan and cool on a cooling rack. Store in a one gallon plastic freezer bag and freeze until one day before the party.

What are Pine Nuts?

Pine nuts are seeds grown in Europe on the Stone Pine (Pinus Pinea). There are two nuts under each cone scale. Pine nuts were discovered over 6,000 years ago. The Swiss Pine (Pinus Cembra) also has pine nuts. However, the Korean Pine (Pinus Koraiensis) is found in northern Asia and this particular pine nut is used the most in international trade. Native American tribes harvest pine nuts, but use them exclusively for their own use. Pine nuts are one of the main ingredients in pesto sauce. They can be eaten with or without salt and also in sweet or savory dishes. A pine nut is about ½ inch long.

Tip
One large orange yields ¼-⅓ cup orange juice. The sweetheart honey bar does not have butter. It is a chewy-style granola bar. Crème bouquet is orange flavoring.

How to Cut the Bars	Number of Bars	Cut Across and Down
8x8 pan	16	4 across x 4 down
9x13 pan	40	5 across x 8 down
11x17 pan	70	7 across x 10 down
16 bars per 8x8 pan	40 bars per 9x13 pan	70 bars per 11x17 pan

Sweetheart Honey Bars
Yield: one 8x8 pan

¾ cup old-fashioned oatmeal
1 cup flour
½ cup wheat germ
½ teaspoon salt
½ teaspoon baking powder
½ teaspoon cinnamon
1 egg, slightly beaten
2 tablespoons sugar
2 tablespoons dark brown sugar
¼ cup honey
1 teaspoon crème bouquet
½ teaspoon grated orange peel,
  optional
¼ cup freshly squeezed orange juice
¼ cup shredded coconut
¼ cup golden raisins
¼ cup pine nuts
no-stick baking spray

Sweetheart Honey Bars
Yield: one 9x13 pan

1½ cups old-fashioned oatmeal
1½ cups flour
¾ cup wheat germ
¾ teaspoon salt
1 teaspoon baking powder
1 teaspoon cinnamon
2 egg, slightly beaten
¼ cup sugar
¼ cup dark brown sugar
½ cup honey
2 teaspoons crème bouquet
1 teaspoon grated orange peel,
  optional
½ cup freshly squeezed orange juice
½ cup shredded coconut
½ cup golden raisins
½ cup pine nuts
no-stick baking spray

In a separate bowl, mix together oatmeal, flour, wheat germ, salt, baking powder and cinnamon. In a second mixing bowl, mix together egg(s), sugar, brown sugar, honey, crème bouquet and orange peel. Beat until smooth and creamy. Alternate the orange juice with the dry ingredients, beginning and ending with the orange juice. Fold in the coconut, raisins and pine nuts. Spray pan with no-stick baking spray. Place batter into the appropriate size pan. Bake at 350F for 20-30 minutes or until toothpick inserted in the center of the bars comes out clean. Cool and frost bars with glaze on page 108.

Sweetheart Honey Bars
Yield: one 11x17 pan

2¼ cups old-fashioned oatmeal
2¼ cups flour
1 cup wheat germ
1 teaspoon salt
1½ teaspoons baking powder
1½ teaspoons cinnamon

3 eggs slightly beaten
½ cup sugar
½ cup dark brown sugar
¾ cup honey
3 teaspoons crème bouquet
2 teaspoons orange peel, optional
¾ cup freshly squeezed orange juice
1 cup shredded coconut
1 cup golden raisins
1 cup pine nuts
no-stick baking spray

In a medium size bowl, mix oatmeal, flour, wheat germ, salt, baking powder and cinnamon. In a five quart mixing bowl, add the eggs, sugar, brown sugar, honey, crème bouquet, orange peel and beat together. Alternately, add the orange juice and dry ingredients, starting and ending with the orange juice. Fold in coconut, raisins and pine nuts. Spray an 11x17 inch pan with no-stick baking spray. Place batter into an 11x17 inch pan. Bake at 350F for 30-40 minutes or until toothpick inserted in the center of the bars come out clean. Cool and frost bars with glaze.

Tip

Heart confetti sprinkles come in a 2.5-ounce jar. There are approximately 6 tablespoons of confetti to one 2.5-ounce jar.

Sweetheart Honey Bar Glaze
Yield: glaze for one 8x8 inch pan

1½ cups powdered sugar
3 tablespoons water
¾ teaspoon coconut flavoring
pinch of salt
1 drop pink food coloring
2 tablespoons heart confetti
  sprinkles

Sweetheart Honey Bar Glaze
Yield: glaze for one 13x9 inch pan

3½ cups powdered sugar
6 tablespoons water
1 teaspoon coconut flavoring
⅛ teaspoons salt
2 drops pink food coloring
5 tablespoons heart confetti
  sprinkles

Sweetheart Honey Bar Glaze
Yield: glaze for one 11x17 pan

6 cups powdered sugar
½ cup water
1½ teaspoon coconut flavoring
¼ teaspoon salt
3 drops pink food coloring
5 tablespoons heart confetti sprinkles

Blend the water into the powdered sugar. Add the coconut flavoring, salt and
Blend the water into the powdered sugar. Add the coconut flavoring, salt and
food coloring. Mix together until mixture is smooth. Spread the glaze over the
bars. Decorate with heart confetti sprinkles. Cut into 70 bars and serve on a
three-tier serving tray. (See illustration on page 83).

Tip
One 19.5 ounce box fudge brownie mix makes one 13x9 pan of brownies and two 19.5
ounce boxes of brownie mix make a 11x17 inch pan.. The cheesecake brownies contain
applesauce and egg whites to reduce fats and calories. One large egg equals one-fourth
cup. One 16-ounce can classic chocolate frosting will frost one 11x17 pan of brownies
and three-fourths of a can will frost a 9x13 pan. Cover each pan of brownies with a
thin layer of icing. Decorate brownies with jimmies or unwrapped candy kisses.(one per
bar) See on page 106. The diagram and information on how to cut bars for the different
size pans. Cheesecake brownie mixes are also sold at the grocery store in 15.5 ounce
boxes. Each box only makes an 8x8 pan of brownies or 12 cup cakes. Follow the box
mix directions for best results.

Cheesecake Brownies
Yield: one 9x13 pan

1-19.5 ounce box brownie mix
⅓ cup applesauce
1 tablespoon water
3 egg whites
1-8 ounce package Neufchatel cheese
 softened(1½ 8-ounce packages)
2 tablespoons Splenda® or ¼ cup
 sugar

Cheesecake Brownies
Yield: one 11x17 pan

2-19.5 ounce boxes (each) brownie mix
2/3 cups applesauce
2 tablespoons water
6 egg whites
12 ounces Neufchatel cheese,
 softened(1½ 8-ounce packages)
3 tablespoons Splenda® or 6
 tablespoon sugar

Cheesecake Brownies ingredients, continued

3 tablespoons flour	6 tablespoons flour
½ teaspoon vanilla	1 teaspoon vanilla
1 egg	2 eggs
no-stick baking spray	no-stick baking spray
¾ of a 16 ounce can cream classic chocolate frosting	1-16 ounce can cream classic chocolate frosting

In a 5 quart mixer, add applesauce and egg whites to the appropriate size brownie batter. Blend batter until smooth. Spray pan with no-stick baking spray. Evenly spread brownie batter into the pan. Beat the Neufchatel cheese and add the sugar or Splenda®, flour, vanilla, and egg(s); beat until smooth. Spoon Neufchatel cheese mixture over the brownies, three spoonfuls across and three down for a 9x13 pan and 3 across and 3 down for a 11x17 pan. Marble the brownies with a metal spatula using an up and down motion. Bake at 350F for 30-40 minutes for a 9x13 pan and 40-45 minutes for an 11x17 pan or until toothpick inserted 2 inches from the side of the pan comes out almost clean. Cool thoroughly on a cooling rack. Frost with chocolate frosting. Place bars on a three-tier serving tray or on a mirror or serving tray of choice.

How to Spoon Neufchatel Cheese Mixture Over the Brownie Batter

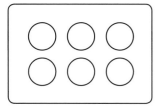

9x13 pan-2 across and 3 down (using 3 down (using a back and forth motion) to marble the brownies

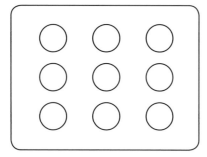

11x17 pan 3 across and 3 down (using a back a back and forth motion) to marble the brownies

Using a back and forth motion marble the brownie batter.

Clay flowerpots must be lined with foil when baking cakes in the pots. Do not place batter into a greased flowerpot for it is not safe unless it is glazed. Line flowerpots with foil for best results. See instructions below on the next page. One-16 ounce can of chocolate frosting will frost 8 flowerpot cakes. There are 45 cookies in a 1 pound 2-ounce package of Oreo® cookies. Crush one Oreo® cookie per flowerpot. Refrigerate decorated flowerpot cakes until the date of the party. The flowerpot cakes can be made 2-3 days in advance of the party.

Use flowerpot centerpieces for individual gifts at each place setting. The flowerpots can be used as an ice breaker. Using several different flavors of cake mixes, vary the flowerpot cakes. Be sure to mark the flavor of each cake on the bottom of each flowerpot.

Invite guests to try to guess the flavor of the cake at each place setting. Each guest can try to trade her cake for another guest's cake at any of the guest tables. The guests will interact with each other and also create great conversation.

Flowerpot Cake Centerpieces
Yield: 6 flowerpot cakes

6 clay flowerpots (4½ inches in diameter,
  4 inches tall)
6-4 inch clay saucers
1-18.5 ounce chocolate cake mix
3 eggs
oil
water
no-stick cooking spray
6-12x16 inch pieces (each)
  heavy duty foil
1-16 ounce can creamy home-style
  classic frosting
6 Oreo® cookies, crushed
6 iris silk flowers (8 inches tall)
6 yards gold 1½ inch ribbon
18-1 inch pieces Scotch® tape

A Flowerpot Cake Centerpiece

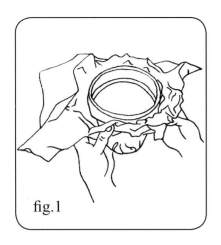

fig.1

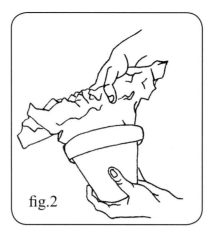

fig.2

fig.3

fig.4

fig.5

Steps on Assembling Flowerpot Cake Centerpiece (fig. 1-5)

Follow the cake box mix directions for mixing batter. For each flowerpot, cut a piece of heavy-duty foil, 12 inches wide and 16 inches long. Place foil around the outside of the pot to form the shape of the pot for each cake (fig.1). Place the shaped foil inside of each pot (fig.2). Slightly roll the edges of the foil under the top of the flowerpot. Spray the inside of the foil with no-stick baking spray. Pour 1 cup of cake batter into the foiled-lined pot, filling to about ⅔ full (fig.3). Bake at 325F for 25-35 minutes or until toothpick inserted into the center of the cake comes out clean. Cool cakes in the flowerpots. Frost the top of each flowerpot cake. Sprinkle one crushed Oreo® cookie over the top of each frosted flowerpot to look like dirt. Place one iris in the center of each baked cake in each pot and 1 yellow cluster flower on each side of the iris (fig.4). Cut 6 one-yard strips of ribbon. Roll the Scotch® tape so it is sticky on both sides. Place one piece of Scotch® tape on the top rim in the center back and one piece centered on each side. Measure and mark at the 18 inches or halfway point of the ribbon. Starting at the back of the pot, place the 18 inch mark or center of ribbon on the Scotch® tape so that the ribbon will not slide off (fig.5). Continue to adhere the ribbon to the tape. The ends of the ribbon should meet. Tie a bow on each pot. Place each flowerpot on a clay saucer.

Flowerpot Cake, continued

How to Cut the Flowerpot Cake

Remove the flowers from the top of the flowerpot cake (fig.1). Remove the cake from the flowerpot (fig.2.). Remove the foil. Starting at the top of the cake, cut in half to make two servings (fig.3). Serve to your sweetheart or a favorite friend over a cup of coffee and great conversation.

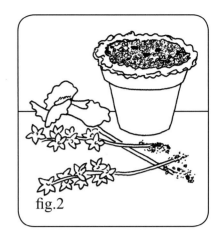
fig.2

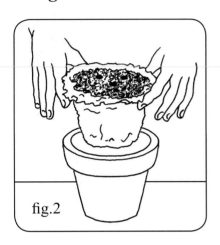
fig.2

fig.3

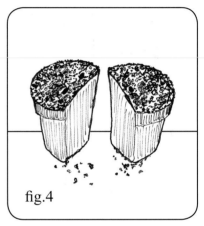
fig.4

Raspberry Iced Tea Detail

Tip

For quick and easy results, use the powdered mix. The pre-sweetened wild raspberry iced tea comes in a 1 pound-12.3 ounce container and each glass contains 80 calories. To make a gallon of wild raspberry tea, mix 1⅓ cups of the powder to 1 gallon of water.

The pre-sweetened raspberry tea mix comes in a 3 pound 5-ounce container and makes 5 gallons. Each glass contains 70 calories.

For best results follow the directions on each container of iced tea mix.

Generally, I figure 2 glasses of iced tea per person if I am not serving any other beverages. I also have water available for the guests. Several people may want coffee with their dessert. I will usually put on a pot of coffee to accommodate those guests. If it is a very warm day, most people will be happy with iced tea and water.

The cost is higher when buying bottled water and bottled iced tea. However, the advantage is that the beverages are ready and saves the hostess preparation time. The bottled water and iced tea can be placed into a cooler with ice and the guests can help themselves. This type of service is very appropriate for a casual party, but, for an elegant party, the ice tea and water should be served in glassware at each guest table.

Measurement Chart for Raspberry Iced Tea Yield

2 cups=1 pint
4 cups=1 quart
8 cups=2 quarts
12 cups=3 quarts
16 cups=1 gallon
4 quarts=1 gallon

Black Cherries

Place black cherries into a clear glass bowl. Figure 6 black cherries per person.

A Bowl of Black Cherries

Grandma Kay's Buffet Setup

Looking at the setup from left to right, cover the buffet with a gold tablecloth.

1. 6 inch plates for appetizers
2. Left corner-arranged vase of flowers
3. In front of the arranged flowers is a tray adorned with birds holding the ham roll-ups.
4. To the right of ham roll-ups is the plate with the crab cake appetizers.
5. Behind the crab cake appetizers is the cool lime sauce.
6. Next to the crab appetizers is a rectangular dish with the turkey croissants.
7. One mayonnaise dish is in front of the turkey croissants.
8. Tomato slices are in back of the brunch bake on a riser. The riser is covered with a gold table cloth.
9. In the center of the buffet is a long tall riser (20 inches long and 9 inches high). A small purple tablecloth covers the riser. The frog is in the center of the riser with one flowerpot on each side of the frog.
10. Three flowerpots with flowers are evenly spaced in front of the riser.
11. Four sets of flower decorations are in front of the flowerpots.
12. To the right of the riser is a hat with sliced bread.
13. To the right of the first hat is the 6th flowerpot.
14. To the right of the flowerpot is the celebration salad with the bird of paradise and seven 3-inch long and ¾ inch thick apple wedges.
15. The second hat is placed at a slight angle on the left of the celebration salad.

16. Soup spoons are to the right of the hat.
17. The soup bowls are to the left of the tureen filled with tomato basil soup.
18. A three tiered dessert tray is holding the brownies with the candy kisses.
19. In front of the bars is a tray of black cherries.
20. Next to the dessert bars is a bouquet of assorted colorful flowers. (See illustration on page 83).

Grandma Kay's Guest Table Setup

Each table is set up for 6 guests. Grandma Kay's colors are gold and purple. Cover the guest table with a gold tablecloth. Each place setting has the following setup:

1. Dinner plate
2. To the left of the plate is a dinner fork.
3. To the left of the dinner fork is a salad fork.
4. To the right of the dinner plate is a knife with the sharp side placed toward the plate.
5. To the right of the knife is a spoon.
6. To the right of the spoon is the coffee cup and saucer.
7. Above the tip of the knife is a water glass.
8. Above the plate is a flowerpot.
9. The purple cloth napkin, adorned with the flowers and silver napkin holder, is placed at a slight slant across the plate.
10. The center of the table has a centerpiece.

Grandma Kay's Guest Table Setup

The 9 Hole Breakfast

Hole		Par	Reds	Whites	Blues	Score
1	Uncle Carl's Breakfast Buffet	4	348	359	370	
2	Orange Juice	4	374	384	394	
3	Sweet Rolls	3	98	114	123	
4	Buttermilk Pancakes with blueberries or pecans -made to order -	4	266	276	286	
5	Breakfast Sausage Links	4	264	275	295	
6	Bacon	4	336	344	352	
7	Decorated Golf Cake	3	101	150	161	
8	Coffee, Cream and Sugar	4	313	322	331	
9	Bottled Water	5	478	488	498	
Total		35	2578	2712	2810	

Grandpa Ray's Bachelor Party

The family was not sure what to do with Ray while the bridal shower was in progress. Uncle Carl came to the rescue especially since he learned that Ray loved to golf and eat pancakes. He volunteered to host a pancake breakfast for Ray at his bachelor's pad. After breakfast the men planned to go to the Treasure Island Golf Course and hopefully play 18 holes.

Grandma Kay did not know much about golf, so Uncle Carl filled her in about the game. Grandma Kay also talked to Uncle Carl about having things decorated nicely for the party. Her granddaughter, Emily, told Grandma Kay not to worry. She would help Uncle Carl. She made golf pattern tablecloths to fit the 4 card tables and borrowed 16 card table chairs for the gathering.

The centerpiece is made using a 7 inch tall glass cylinder candleholder, 20 inches in circumference. The candleholder sits up on an attached 1½ inches tall stem on a round base, 16 inches in circumference. Each candle holder holds 36 golf balls, which Uncle Carl loaned Emily for the occasion. In the center of each is a plastic golfer, swinging his club and attached to a stick, which is inserted down through the golf balls.

Above the center of each place setting is a footed clear glass compote dish filled with 8 ounces of wrapped chocolate golf balls. Any stemmed glassware such as a goblet, Margarita glass or martini glass can be substituted for the footed compote and filled with an adjusted amount of candy. A golf flag on a pole is placed into the center of each favor. In addition, each place setting has a fork, knife, spoon, napkin with napkin ring and a cut crystal juice glass.

Grandpa Ray's Guest Table Setup

How to Decorate the Footed Compote Glass
Yield: 1 party favor

42 inches green ribbon
2 tees
1 flag or golfer
½ pound wrapped
  miniature chocolate
 golf balls
1 footed compote
  glass, 5 inches in diameter
  with a 3 inch tall stem

Cut ribbon. Fold ribbon in half to make 21 inches. Fold ribbon in half again to make 10½ inches. Tie a double knot around the bottom of the stem of the compote-footed glass to form a bow. Crisscross two tees and place through the knot to look like an x. The x stands for a kiss. Cut each ribbons loop in half lengthwise. The candy will fill the compote glass half full. Place the flag or golfer in the center of the compote glass. (See illustration on page 120).

Tip
The chart below gives the amounts needed for the number of favors at the party.

Chart for Each Glass Compote Favor

Ribbon	Compote Glasses	Compote Glasses
number of glasses	4 compote glasses	8 compote glasses
yards of ribbon	4¾ yards	9½ yards
number of glasses	12 compote glasses	16 compote glasses
yards of ribbon	14¼ yards	19 yards

Tip
Four tees come per package. One package will decorate two compote glasses. I purchased the packages of tees at my local cake-decorating store.

Golfer Flag

1 golfer or flag per footed compote glass (your choice)

Chart for Chocolate Golf Balls (½ Pound per Glass)

1 table	2 pounds for four people, divided
2 tables	4 pounds for eight people, divided
3 tables	6 pounds for 12 people, divided
4 tables	8 pounds for 16 people, divided

How to Decorate the Napkin Ring and Napkin Detail
Yield: one napkin ring

1 wooden napkin ring
1 tee
1 miniature golf ball
hot glue stick
hot glue gun

Hot glue miniature golf ball into the little indentation on the tee area. Hot glue the green tee-shaped area to the napkin ring and the flag to the little hole on the green tee. Fold napkin in half lengthwise and three even lengths the short way. Roll up the napkin like a diploma and slide it through the napkin ring. Make sure that the green tee shaped area is standing up on the napkin ring. The napkin ring with the napkin is placed to the left of the dinner fork. (See illustration on page 120).

Grandpa Ray's Place Setting
Yield: 1 hat and 1 badge

1 "Number 1 Golfer" badge
1 decorated hat

Grandpa Ray is wearing the badge and the decorated gold hat. (See illustration on page 120).

How to Decorate Grandpa Ray's Special Golfer's Hat

1 soft hat with brim and 6-1¾
  width wide loops spaced around the
  crown of the hat
1 strip of golf print material, 33 inches long and 5 inches wide

Pink the raw edges of the fabric. Fold the material in half lengthwise and repeat to form a 1½ inch wide long band. Starting at the front, weave the material through each loop on the hat. At the back of the hat, ties ends together and tuck extra material under the band.

For many years Uncle Carl had friends and family come to his bachelor's pad for his favorite menu. He said, "A cook can't go wrong with this great and simple menu." His favorite food was always buttermilk pancakes. He prepared the food and displayed it on his breakfast bar. He made it clear to the guests that it's a help-yourself setup. He liked to put in at least 2 tablespoons of apple cider vinegar per batch of pancakes. He said that apple cider vinegar in pancakes helped clear the plaque in the veins. Grandma Kay thought that was very strange. She used apple cider vinegar to make her favorite cucumber salad, dressings for salads and sour milk for banana bread. Nevertheless, she respected Uncle Carl's pancake recipe.

Story about Uncle Carl

For many years, cousins Marie and Max, along with extended family Sadie and Sam, came to Uncle Carl's condo for breakfast. One year, upon their arrival, Uncle Carl announced that he was going to be doing some remodeling of his bachelor's pad. Since he retired, he could take his time to refinish the kitchen cabinets. As they were sitting around and talking, he showed them a sample of the countertop. Sadie said, "Oh no, not periwinkle. That surely will not match your kitchen colors." Uncle Carl looked at Max and Max looked at Carl. Uncle Carl then asked, "What is periwinkle?" Sadie said, "It is in the blue family." At that point, Sadie volunteered to help Uncle Carl coordinate the colors for his kitchen countertops. She also coordinated the paint, color of cupboards and floor to make a beautiful and functional kitchen. Uncle Carl tells this story to all new visitors while eating his favorite buttermilk pancakes.

Sweet rolls come 10 to a 12.4 ounce can. The directions on the can show how to make a coffee cake or place rolls individually on a baking sheet. Uncle Carl prefers to bake the sweet rolls on a cookie sheet. He places the frosted sweet rolls on a tray and usually serves them first with coffee while the guests are waiting for the main meal. Everyone works up an appetite from the fantastic aroma of the pancakes and the bacon. He generally pours glasses of orange juice last so that the juice stays cold. Emily owns individual miniature brandy snifters. She fills them with maple syrup and sets them out, one for every place setting. Of course, she has extra syrup for refills. Uncle Carl usually makes up small batches of pancakes with all the dry ingredients ahead of time. He adds the liquid ingredients for each batch on the day of the party. Once the griddle is hot, he feels it is easy to continue to make several batches of pancakes. Sometimes he adds 1 tablespoon of blueberries or chopped pecans over each pancake when the pancakes become bubbly and before he flips them to cook on the other side.

Before Uncle Carl started to make up the pancake batter, he began to think about Granma Kay's strong opinion on not using vinegar in buttermilk pancakes. He decided to omit the vinegar in the recipe to please her.

Uncle Carl's Buttermilk Pancakes
Yield: 10 pancakes

1¼ cups all-purpose flour
2 teaspoons sugar
½ teaspoon baking powder
½ teaspoon baking soda
¼ teaspoon salt
2 eggs
1¼ cups buttermilk
1 tablespoon butter, melted
1 teaspoon vanilla
1 quart maple syrup

Combine flour, sugar, baking powder, baking soda, and salt in a mixing bowl. Add the eggs, buttermilk, butter and vanilla to the flour mixture. Mix ingredients together until slightly lumpy. Heat griddle to 375F. When water sprinkled on the griddle dances, the griddle is hot enough to make pancakes. Place 10 four inch round pancakes on the griddle. Turn each pancake when edges are slightly dry and the surface of the pancake is bubbly (about 2 minutes per side). Serve with butter and warm maple syrup.

Uncle Carl's Breakfast Setup

Uncle Carl made the bacon on his indented square fry pan because the grease runs down into the indentation and frees the bacon grease from the bacon. After frying each batch, he drains the grease into a can. He places the cooked bacon on a paper towel and keeps it in a warm oven until serving time. He figures a pound of bacon feeds five people and also cooks 2 breakfast sausage links per person. He cooks the sausage in a little water on medium heat on top of the stove. When sausages are cooked through, he browns the sausages. He places the sausages on a platter and keeps them warm in the oven until serving time. He makes a pot of decaf and a pot of regular coffee to please the crowd. Since the shower he has informed our family that he now has a new method of cooking bacon. He purchased parchment paper 15 inches wide and 2 aluminum foil throw away pans the size of the parchment paper. He lines the 2 pans with the parchment paper and places a pound of bacon strips on each lined pan. He bakes the bacon at 375F for 10-12 minutes on one side. He removes the bacon from the oven and drains the grease. Next, he turns the bacon over and places the bacon back into the oven and bakes it for 10-12 more minutes. He is very pleased with his new method for he feels the bacon comes out very straight and nice and crisp.

How to Set Up the Pancake Breakfast Buffet
On Uncle Carl's Breakfast Bar Starting Left to Right

1. Container with bottles of water
2. Coffee pot
3. Coffee mugs
4. Green cocktail napkins
5. Leave space on the kitchen countertop so people can watch Uncle Carl make the pancakes.
6. Ray's surprise birthday cake bachelor party cake on the corner of the bar
7. The sweet rolls platter has a brandy snifter holding a golf ball and placed in the center of the plate.

Ray arrived a little early for the party. Uncle Carl greeted him and said, "Come on in and make yourself comfortable." As Ray approached the living room, he immediately noticed the wolf picture collection. He asked Uncle Carl if he could see the pictures. Uncle Carl took him on a tour and elaborated on each picture. Ray told Uncle Carl that he also has several wolf pictures.

Eventually all the guests arrived. Uncle Carl was very pleasant and welcoming. Everyone enjoyed the breakfast and was very much at ease. Many of the guests did not know each other, but became fast friends by the end of the breakfast and golf outing.

Before they headed out for the golf course, Uncle Carl presented Ray with a surprise birthday cake decorated in a golf theme. (See Illustration on page 125).

Tip

One set of golf cake decorations has the following items in a 13 piece set:
One male golfer, 4½ inches high
Three tees, 2 inches across
Three miniature golf balls, ¼ inch in diameter
Three flags (1 red, 1 blue, 1 yellow) 3 inches long
Three golf clubs, 5 inches long

Wilton Cake Supply sells the golf set. Check out their website www.wilton..com

How to Make the Golf Cake
Yield: one 9x13 inch cake

1-18.25 ounce package
  yellow cake mix
3 eggs
water
canola oil
no-stick baking spray
10x14 inch cake decorative cardboard
16x18 inch cake platter

Mix the cake per package directions. Spray the 9x13 pan with no-stick cooking spray. Place cake batter into the pan. Bake at 350F for 30-35 minutes or until toothpick inserted in the center comes out clean. Cool for about five minutes. Turn the cake out of the baking pan onto the cardboard. Cool thoroughly. Place a dab of frosting in the middle of the16x18 inch tray. Place the cake onto the tray. Frost the cake with the butter cream frosting.

Butter Cream Frosting
Yield: 1 golf cake (16 pieces)

½ cup butter, softened
½ cup shortening
1 teaspoon almond extract
2 pounds powdered sugar
⅓ cup water
½ teaspoon salt
green food coloring

How to Decorate the Golf Cake
Yield: one 9x13 inch decorated golf cake

1 roll of golf print wrapping paper
1-4x5 inch plastic circle
6 golf ball candles
1 golfer
2 sets (each) 1 plastic green turfs
  golf clubs
1 roll golf print wrapping paper
Scotch® Tape

Beat butter and shortening together. Add the almond extract and the water alternately with the powdered sugar. Beat until smooth and creamy. Add 4-5 drops of green food coloring to the frosting and beat until the color is the same throughout the frosting. Using a number 234 cake tube, create a grass like effect on the top and sides of the cake. Cut out a 4x5 inch wide half circle out of a plastic non-dairy whipped topping lid. Place the side with no writing facing up in the center of the cake. With a number 7 writing tip, write "You're a par above the rest." Crisscross two sets of cake decorating golf clubs and place one set at the left and right hand corners of the cake.

golfer. Place three golf ball candles on each side of the golfer. Place a couple of the green turfs with flag and golf ball slightly above and off center of the writing on the cake. Fitting the paper around the sides of the cake platter cut and tape all four sides of the cake platter with the golf print paper. The paper should butt up against the cake. (See illustration on page 125).

A Note to Uncle Carl

You are a lifesaver,
By doing this favor.

You've got what it takes,
When making delicious pancakes.

You are the gracious host,
Always giving the most.

You are our star,
The best uncle by far.

Always taking life in stride,
Entertaining with great pride

Spending time to help Grandma Kay,
You have made Grandpa Ray and everyone's day.

Thank you!!!

Love,
Emily and Family

A France Destination Party Menu

Appetizers

Assorted Cheese
Gourmet Crackers
Raw Vegetables
French Onion Dip

Beverages

Wine, Sodas, Water

Elegant Luncheon

Crab and Artichoke Quiche
Ham and Asparagus Roll ups
with Hollandaise Sauce
Dill Potato Salad
Green Beens Almondine
Spinach and Romaine Berry Salad
with Orange Honey Dressing
French Bread and Butter
Chocolate Fountain with
Strawberries, Bananas, Pineapple, Angel Food Cake,
Donut Holes, Marshmallows, and Pretzels

Casual Luncheon

Menu 1	Menu 2
French Onion Soup	Pat's Favorite French Onion Soup
Assorted Crackers	Assorted Crackers
Chef Salad and Dressing	Salad Nicoise
French Bread and Butter	French Bread and Butter
Dessert Crepes or	French Pear Tart or
Chocolate Fondue and Dippers	Chocolate Raspberry Pear Tart

Chapter 7
Paris is for Lovers Bridal Shower Theme

The party was created for a very special couple. They each waited for a long time to meet that special person and the clock was ticking. Both were 35 years old and had never been married. Chris tried a dating service for a year and felt he was getting nowhere. Nanci had thought long and hard about using a dating service. She went to the library to use the computer and signed up for the same dating service as Chris. Within her first month, she received a response from Chris. To get acquainted, they decided to meet at a local restaurant for their first date. They had a wonderful evening and both wanted to meet again. Chris told Nanci he was taking a trip to France and would be gone for two weeks. While he was in France, he emailed her daily. Upon his return, he took her out to dinner to tell her all about his trip. While they were eating, a stranger came up to them and asked them how long they had been married. They smiled and gave the stranger a fictitious story. They told her they had flown to Paris and Chris had proposed at sunset. The lady never caught on that this was only Chris and Nanci's second date.

Nanci not only taught school, but also worked for a local merchant. Her boss sent her an invitation to his parent's 50th wedding anniversary party. The invitation included a guest. Nanci invited Chris and again, they had a wonderful time. They enjoyed being together very much and, after 8 months of dating, had fallen deeply in love.

Chris decided to propose on April 24th. He went to her school principal and arranged to have a substitute teacher come in that morning. When Nanci arrived at school, she found a pink rose and note from Chris. "I hope today will be the beginning of a very special day for both of us. I have arranged for a substitute teacher. You will be getting a series of cards to tell you where to go. The second card should not be opened until 11:00 a.m. I know that devotional time is very important to you, so find a quiet place to be with the Lord." He also told her the pink rose was for her beauty and gentle personality. "Go to the local restaurant where we met for our first date and ask for Robin."

Nanci did so and Robin led her to a table where she found a red rose and two more cards. All the while, music was playing to remind Nanci of their first date. The first of the two cards said that the red rose symbolized the strength of their relationship and celebrated her coming into Chris's life.* He would not be joining her for lunch and told her not to open the other card until 11:50 a.m. After lunch, she opened the other card, which sent her to a spa. There she had a massage, manicure, hair styling along with another card. This card directed her to meet Chris at the end of the trail at the park. Lining the path were white, red, and pink roses and candles. Chris met Nanci and gave her a white rose. He got down on bended knee and proposed. She accepted and they dined at the French restaurant where Chris had made reservations. While planning their wedding they knew they could not afford to fly to Paris for their honeymoon so co-workers gave Nanci and Chris a beautiful wedding shower with a French theme. One year after meeting, almost to the date, they were married and are a very happy couple.

 * Chris used different colors of roses to express his feelings for Nanci. See the color chart on page 219 to learn more about the colors of love.

Assorted Cheese Board

Tip

Do not feel that you need a big variety of cheese especially if you have a small group. When serving 12 people use only two types of cheese. When serving 24 people use four types of cheese. I often find that a cheese ball is nice for a smaller group. Red and green grapes are ideal for garnishing the cheese ball or cheese platter. One and a half pound cheese ball serves 12 people. Sometimes I purchase a ready-to-serve cheese ball and place it in the center of a 12-inch serving tray. I add a pound of sliced salami and serve it with a pound of crackers of my choice.

Assorted Cheese Board
With Gourmet Crackers
Yield: 50-60 servings

1 pound cranberry Chardonnay
  cheddar
¾ pound Merlot cheddar
²/₃ cups unsalted roasted peanuts
1 pound Brie cheese
¾ pound Raclette Livradoux cheese
1 pound Havarti Cheese
¾ pound French Gourmandise
  with Kirsh
1 pound Edam cheese
¾ pound smoked string cheese
8 pieces endive
½ bunch parsley
¾ pound red grapes
¾ pound green grapes
1-10x22 inch cheese board or
  tray of choice

French Bread and Cheese Board

Form the cranberry Chardonnay cheese into a ball. Place the nuts on a piece of waxed paper. Roll the cheese ball into the nuts covering the entire cheese ball. Arrange the cheese ball, Merlot cheddar, Brie, Raclette Livradoux, Havarti, French Gourmandise with Kirsh, Edam, and smoked string cheese. Garnish with endive, parsley, and red and green grapes. (See photo on page 132 and above).

French Bread and Gourmet Crackers
Yield: 50 servings

2 loaves French bread, sliced
3 pounds gourmet crackers
Arrange the French bread in a basket and crackers on a tray.

Assorted Cheese Board Arrangement

1. **Front left Merlot cheddar**
2. **Front right cranberry Chardonnay cheddar**
3. **Smoked string cheese in between the Merlot cheddar and cranberry Chardonnay cheddar**
4. **red grapes, endive**
5. **Center-wheel of Brie cheese with parsley around the Brie Cheese and green grape garnish top of the Brie cheese**
6. **Behind the brie on the right side is the Havarti cheese.**
7. **Left side Edam cheese**
8. **Right side Gourmandize with Kirsch**
9. **The string cheese is between the Edam and French Gourmandize cheese with Kirsch.**

Tip
One pound of cauliflower will yield a ½ pound of flowerets and the remainder in waste. One pound of broccoli will yield a ½ pound of flowerets and the remainder in waste.

Raw Vegetables	Raw Vegetables	Raw Vegetables
Yield: 12 servings	**Yield: 20-24 servings**	**Yield: 50 servings**
¾ pound baby carrots	1¼ pounds baby carrots	2½ pounds baby carrots
1 pound grape tomatoes	1½ pounds grape tomatoes	3 pounds grape tomatoes
1 pound broccoli flowerets	2 pounds broccoli flowerets	4½ pounds broccoli flowerets
1 pound cauliflower flowerets	2 pounds cauliflower flowerets	4½ pounds cauliflower flowerets
1-12 inch tray	1-16 inch tray	2-12 inch trays

Clean and cut the vegetables and arrange on a tray(s). Serve with French onion dip.

Tip
There are 2-1 ounce packages of onion soup mix per 2.0 ounce box.

French Onion Dip
Yield: 10-12 servings

1-8 ounce package
  Neufchatel cheese,
  softened
1 cup light sour cream
1 cup plain yogurt
1-1 ounce package
  onion soup mix
1 small bowl

French Onion Dip
Yield: 20-24 servings

2-8 ounce packages
  (each) Neufchatel
  cheese, softened
2 cups light sour cream
2 cups plain yogurt
2-1 ounce packages (each)
  onion soup mix
1 medium bowl

French Onion Dip
Yield: 50 servings

3-8 ounce packages
  (each) Neufchatel
  cheese, softened
3 cups light sour cream
3 cups plain yogurt
3-1 ounce packages (each)
  onion soup mix
1 large bowl

Beat Neufchatel cheese until smooth and creamy. Add sour cream, yogurt and the onion soup mix. Continue to beat all ingredients together until creamy. Refrigerate until serving time. Serve with the raw vegetables.

Tip

When making several quiches, double the recipe twice and use the assembly line method. I personally like to make two to three different kinds of quiche for the guests. Not everyone likes crab or artichoke hearts.

Crab Quiche
Yield: 8 servings

1-9 inch pie crust
1-8 ounce package
  cream cheese,
  softened
¼ cup plain yogurt
4 eggs, beaten
1-6 ounce can
  white crab meat, rinsed
  and drained
½ teaspoon lemon juice
¼ cup red onions, diced
1-14 ounce can
  quartered artichoke
  hearts, chopped

Crab Quiche
Yield: 16 servings

2-9 inch pie crusts
2-8 ounce packages
  (each) cream cheese,
  softened
⅓ cup plain yogurt
8 eggs, beaten
2-6 ounce cans (each)
  white crab meat, rinsed
  and drained
1 teaspoon lemon juice
⅓ cup red onions, diced
1½ -14 ounce cans (each)
  quartered artichoke
  hearts, chopped

Crab Quiche
Yield: 24 servings

3-9 inch pie crusts
3-8 ounce packages
  (each) cream cheese,
  softened
½ cup plain yogurt
12 eggs, beaten
3-6 ounce cans (each)
  white crab meat, rinsed
  and drained
1½ teaspoons lemon juice
½ cup red onions, diced
2-14 ounce cans (each)
  quartered artichoke
  hearts, chopped

Crab Quiche, continued

¼ cup mushrooms, diced	⅓ cup mushrooms, diced	½ cup mushrooms, diced
¼ cup celery, diced	⅓ cup celery, diced	½ cup celery, diced
½ teaspoon white pepper	¾ teaspoon white pepper	1 teaspoon white pepper
1 cup semi-soft Colby cheese, divided	2 cups semi-soft Colby cheese, divided	3 cups semi-soft Colby cheese, divided

Beat cream cheese until smooth. Add yogurt, eggs, crab meat, lemon juice, red onions, artichoke hearts, mushrooms, celery, white pepper and half of the Colby cheese. Pour mixture into the pie shell(s). Sprinkle the remaining cheese over the top of each quiche. Bake at 375F for 40-45 minutes or until golden brown and toothpick inserted in the center comes out clean. (See photo).

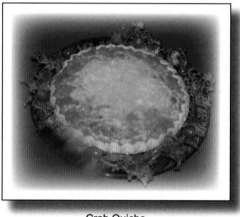
Crab Quiche

Ham and Asparagus Roll-Ups
Yield: 12 servings

2 cups all-purpose baking mix
²/₃ cup milk
12 slices baked ham
¾ pound shredded Swiss cheese
2 cups water
36 pieces asparagus
½ cup yellow mustard
2 tablespoon horseradish sauce
1 tablespoon dehydrated minced onion
1 teaspoon dehydrated minced garlic
1 tablespoon poppy seed
4 tablespoons butter, melted
3 tablespoons flour

Ham and Asparagus Roll-Ups
Yield: 24 servings

4 cups all-purpose baking mix
1 ⅓ cups milk
24 slices baked ham
1½ pounds shredded Swiss cheese
4 cups water
72 pieces asparagus
1 cup yellow mustard
4 tablespoons horseradish sauce
2 tablespoons dehydrated minced onion
2 teaspoons dehydrated minced garlic
2 teaspoons poppy seed
8 tablespoons butter, melted
6 tablespoons flour

Stir together the baking mix and milk. Dust the cutting board with flour. Place biscuit dough on cutting board and knead until lightly firm. Roll out dough to ¹/₈ inch thick. Using a 3½ inch cookie cutter, cut out 12-24 pieces. Continue to roll out dough into approximately 6 inch circles. Set aside. Place asparagus into a

Ham and Asparagus Roll-Ups, continued
large pan with 2-4 cups water, depending on a 12 or 24 size batch. Bring to a boil and cook only until asparagus is barely tender. Drain and rinse the asparagus in cold water; set aside. Mix together the mustard, horseradish sauce, minced onions, garlic and poppy seed. Divide the mustard sauce evenly.

Steps in Assembling Ham and Asparagus Roll-Ups (fig. 1-6)

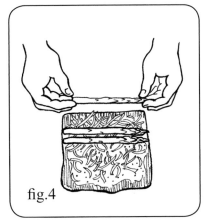

fig.1

Roll out the dough.

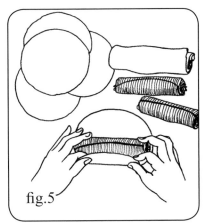

fig.2

Spread sauce over each piece of ham.

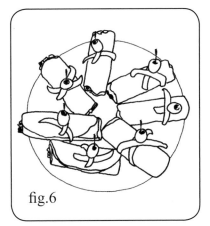

fig.3

Place Swiss cheese over ham.

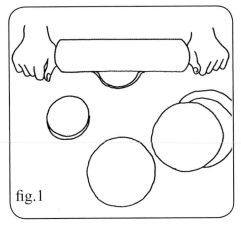

fig.4

Place three pieces of asparagus lengthwise on the edge of each ham slice.

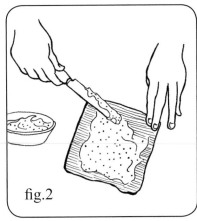

fig.5

Roll up the ham; wrap on 6x6 inch piece of dough around each ham roll-up.

fig.6

Lightly brush butter over the roll-ups.

Bake at 350F for 12-15 minutes or until golden brown.

Suggested Garnishes for Ham and Asparagus Roll-Ups:

One green and red pepper slice to form an X and a green olive for the O with a frilled toothpick pierced through the middle of the olive and through the pepper X. Pierce each asparagus roll-up with garnish. See illustration (fig.6). Another garnish suggestion is a frilled toothpick with a cucumber slice and a black olive.

Tip

Biscuits, or crescent rolls in a can may be used to cover the ham and asparagus roll-ups as an alternative to mixing biscuit dough. There are 10 biscuits and 8 crescent triangles to a can. However, using 2 triangles make one square, pressing seam together for each roll-up. One can of biscuits covers 10 roll-ups and 4 crescent squares cover 4 ham and asparagus roll-ups. Crêpes are also a good basic batter for making the roll-ups. You can make crêpes one or two days before the party; refrigerate and fill crêpes on day of the party. Six-inch soft taco shells can also be used to make the roll-ups to eliminate the step of rolling out dough to save time.

Other Types of Dough Used for the Ham and Asparagus Roll -Ups

Puff Pastry
Yield: 8 rolls-ups

1-17.3 ounces box puff pastry

Roll out each of the two sheets of puff pastry to a 12x12 in square. Cut four 6x6 inch squares from each sheet. Using the filling recipe on page 137, place 1 ham roll-up on the edge of the puff pastry and roll the dough around the ham roll-up. Pinch the edges of the dough together at each end of the ham roll-up to prevent the cheese from oozing out. Bake at 375F for 12-15 minutes or until golden brown.

Crescent Rolls
Yield: 4 roll ups

2-8 ounce cans (each)
  crescent rolls

Lay out two crescent rolls connected together to form a square. Roll out each square into a 6x6 inch square. Wrap the crescent roll around the ham and asparagus roll-up. Pinch the edges of the dough together to prevent the cheese from oozing out. Bake at 375F for 6-12 minutes or until golden brown.

Canned Biscuits
Yield: 10

Roll out the biscuits on floured board into 6 inch round shapes. Roll the biscuits around the ham and asparagus roll-up. Bake at 350F until biscuit is golden brown and ham roll-up is heated through.

Crêpes Yield: 12	Crêpes Yield: 24
2 cups milk	4 cups milk
2 tablespoons sugar	4 tablespoons sugar
3 eggs	6 eggs
1 teaspoon vanilla	2 teaspoons vanilla
1 cup flour	2 cups flour
2 tablespoons butter, melted	4 tablespoons butter, melted
dash of salt	¼ teaspoon salt

Mix together the milk, sugar, eggs and vanilla. Whisk in the flour a little at a time. Stir in the melted butter and salt into the crêpe batter. On a large griddle with the temperature of 350F, shape two 6 inch round crêpes by spreading ⅓ cup crêpe batter. Use the bottom of the measuring cup to spread out the crêpe evenly into a circle. Loosen the bottom of the crêpe with a long stainless steel cake-decorating spatula. Flip crêpe over with the pancake turner. Remove crêpes one at a time and place each crêpe onto a piece of waxed paper. Cool. When cooled, place waxed paper between each crêpe and stack. Waxed paper between crepes will prevent the crêpes from sticking together. To reheat the crêpe wrap roll-ups, use a broiler pan. Place 1 inch of water in the bottom of the broiler pan. Place top with slits over the broiler pan. Place crêpe ham and asparagus roll-ups on the broiler pan. Bake at 300F for15-20 minutes or until ham roll-ups are heated through. Serve immediately.

The History of Crêpes

The crêpe is considered a French pancake. The word crêpe comes from the Latin word (crispus) meaning that the pancake is flat and slightly crisp in texture. The crêpe originated in Brittany France. To this day they still make sweet crêpes. Many crêpes are made with meats and cheeses. "In Medieval times, peasants presented crêpes to their feudal Lords as a demonstration of loyalty". There is actually a museum in Breton town of Quimper. They celebrate the history of crêpes.

Crêpes came to America in the 1930's by a French Chef Henri Charpentier. He laid claim on being the person that originated the Crêpes Suzettes (serving them to the future King Edward VII in Monte Carlo). Several folks have challenged his claim. Nevertheless, the Crêpes Suzette became a classic dish with its delicious orange sauce. It is the staple feature of haute cuisine in America.

Hollandaise Sauce, continued

yolks until they begin to thicken. Add the water one tablespoon at a time and continue to beat in each tablespoon of water. Add the fresh squeezed lemon juice and continue to beat into the sauce. Whisk in the melted butter a little at a time until blended. Add the salt and cayenne pepper. When the sauce is thick enough, remove from the double boiler and serve at once.

Tip

Drizzle only a little of the Hollandaise sauce over the ham and asparagus roll-ups. Leave a few roll-ups plain.

Dill Potato Salad
Yield: 12 servings (4 pounds)

3 pounds red potatoes
1 bunch scallions, chopped with tops
½ cup celery
½ pound bacon
2 tablespoons dried basil
1 teaspoon dried thyme
¼ cup red bell pepper, diced
¼ cup green bell pepper, diced
1 teaspoon minced garlic
¾ teaspoon salt
½ teaspoon white pepper
½ cup olive oil
¼ cup champagne vinegar
1-0.7 package Good Seasons®
  Italian salad dressing mix
1 tablespoon dill weed
1 tablespoon Dijon mustard

Garnish for Dill Potato Salad
Yield: 12 servings

1 medium bunch parsley, divided
12 grape tomatoes, divided
1 medium serving bowl

Dill Potato Salad
Yield: 20-24 servings (6 pounds)

6 pounds red potatoes
2 bunches scallions, chopped with tops
1 cup celery
¾ pound bacon
3 tablespoons dried basil
1½ teaspoons dried thyme
⅓ cup red bell pepper, diced
⅓ cup green bell pepper, diced
2 teaspoons minced garlic
1 teaspoon salt
¾ teaspoon white pepper
1 cup olive oil
½ cup champagne vinegar
2-0.7 packages (each) Good Seasons®
  Italian salad dressing mix
4 teaspoons dill weed
4 teaspoons Dijon mustard

Garnish for Dill Potato Salad
Yield: 20-24 servings

1 large bunch parsley, divided
20 grape tomatoes, divided
3 medium serving bowls

Dill Potato Salad
Yield: 40 servings (10 pounds)

10 pounds red potatoes
2½ bunches scallions, chopped
  with tops
1¼ cups celery, diced
1½ pounds bacon
2 teaspoons dried basil
1¾ teaspoons dried thyme
¾ cup red bell pepper, diced
¾ cup green bell pepper, diced
1 teaspoon salt
1 teaspoon white pepper
¼ cup minced garlic
1½ cups olive oil
1½ cups champagne vinegar
3-0.7 ounce packages (each) Good
  Seasons® Italian salad dressing mix
¼ cup dill weed
¼ cup Dijon mustard

Dill Potato Salad
Yield: 50 servings (13 pounds)

13 pounds red potatoes
3 bunches scallions, chopped
  with tops
1½ cups celery, diced
1¾ pounds bacon
2½ teaspoons dried basil
2 teaspoons dried thyme
1 cup red bell pepper, diced
1 cup green bell pepper, diced
1½ teaspoons salt
1¼ teaspoons pepper
5 tablespoons minced garlic
2 cups olive oil
2 cups champagne vinegar
4-0.7 ounce packages (each) Good
  Seasons® Italian salad dressing mix
5 tablespoons dill weed
5 tablespoons Dijon mustard

Garnish for Dill Potato Salad
Yield: 40 servings

1 large bunch parsley, divided
30 grape tomatoes
1 medium and 1 large serving bowl

Garnish for Dill Potato Salad
Yield: 50 servings

1 large bunch parsley, divided
1-10 ounce container grape tomatoes
2 large serving bowls

Clean and boil potatoes with skins until fork tender. Drain and cool the potatoes. Quarter or dice each potato, depending on the size. Dice bacon and fry on low heat. Add scallions, and red and green peppers and fry vegetables until barely tender. Remove bacon and vegetables from the frying pan. Drain grease. Dab grease off of the bacon and vegetables with paper towel. Add salt and pepper and dill weed to the potatoes. Mix ingredients together well. In a blender add the olive oil, vinegar, dressing mix and Dijon mustard. Blend salad dressing ingredients well. Pour over the potato mixture and stir until potatoes are coated. Put potato salad into suggested size serving bowl(s) and garnish with parsley and grape tomatoes. (See photo on page 144).

Tip
Each pound of green beans serves 5 people.

Fresh Green Beans with Almonds
Yield: 5 servings

1 pound fresh green beans
6 tablespoons butter, melted
salt and pepper to taste
1 teaspoon lemon juice
¼ cup blanched almonds

Fresh Green Beans with Almonds
Yield 20 servings

5 pounds fresh green beans
1½ cups butter, melted
salt and pepper to taste
1 tablespoon lemon juice
1 cup blanched almonds

Snip the ends of the beans. Rinse off in cold water. Place beans in a medium size pan and add water to barely cover the beans. Bring to a boil and cook until barely tender. Drain off the hot water. Immediately place beans in cold water with ice to stop the beans from cooking. Drain off the ice water and dry beans off with paper towel. Add the butter, salt, pepper, lemon juice and blanched almonds. Reheat the green beans on the day of party. (See photo below).

Tip

Make 10-20 servings of dressing at a time in order to fit the ingredients into a home-style blender. Store the lettuce and spinach in plastic storage bags. Add remaining ingredients on the day of the party.

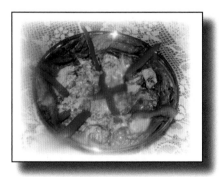

Dill Potato Salad

Fresh Green Beans with Almonds

Spinach and Romaine Berry Salad

Spinach and Romaine Berry Salad with Orange Honey Dressing

Spinach and Romaine Berry Salad
Yield: 10 servings

1-9 ounce package spinach
1 head romaine lettuce, chopped
1 cup raspberries, divided
1 cup blueberries, divided
1 cup strawberries, divided
½ medium red onion, sliced thin

Spinach and Romaine Berry Salad
Yield: 20 servings

2-9 ounce packages (each) spinach
2 heads (each) romaine lettuce, chopped
2 cups raspberries, divided
2 cups blueberries, divided
2 cups strawberries, divided
1 red onion, sliced thin

Spinach and Romaine Berry Salad
Yield: 40 servings

4-9 ounce packages (each) spinach
4 heads romaine lettuce, chopped
4 cups raspberries, divided
4 cups blueberries, divided
4 cups strawberries, divided
1¼ medium onions, sliced thin

Spinach and Romaine Berry Salad
Yield: 50 servings

5-9 ounce packages (each) spinach
5 heads romaine lettuce, chopped
5 cups raspberries, divided
5 cups blueberries, divided
5 cups strawberries, divided
1½ medium onions, sliced thin

Orange Honey Dressing
Yield: 10 servings

1 cup olive oil
½ cup raspberry vinegar
1 fresh orange, peeled
  and cut into segments
⅓ cup honey
2 teaspoons Splenda®
2 tablespoons poppy seeds
1 teaspoon minced garlic

Orange Honey Dressing
Yield: 20 servings

2 cups olive oil
1 cup raspberry vinegar
2 fresh oranges, peeled
  and cut into segments
2/3 cup honey
1 tablespoon Splenda®
3 tablespoons poppy seeds
2 teaspoons minced garlic

Orange Honey Dressing
Yield: 40 servings

3 cups olive oil
1½ cups raspberry vinegar
2½ fresh oranges, peeled
  and cut into segments
4 teaspoons Splenda®
4 teaspoons poppy seeds
3 teaspoons minced garlic

Orange Honey Dressing
Yield: 50 servings

3½ cups olive oil
1¾ cups raspberry vinegar
3 fresh oranges, peeled
  and cut into segments
5 teaspoons Splenda®
5 teaspoons poppy seeds
4 teaspoons minced garlic

Wash the spinach and romaine lettuce. Pat dry. Cut off stems on the fresh spinach leaves. Cut out the centers of the romaine lettuce and cut into bite size pieces. Add half the raspberries, blueberries, strawberries and the onion to the salad. Mix salad together. In a blender, add olive oil, vinegar, oranges, garlic, honey, Splenda®, poppy seed and dehydrated minced garlic. On the day of the party, stir dressing into the salad and toss until well coated. Garnish with remaining fruit. (See photo on page 144).

French Bread and Butter
 Yield: 10 servings

1 loaf French bread
1 stick butter
1 cloth napkin
1 bread basket

Slice French bread and arrange in a basket lined with a cloth napkin. Place butter onto a 6 inch china dish and serve with the bread.

Chocolate Fountain Details

Tip

I use two chocolate fountains when serving a large party. I set up two stations. I like using a round table for each station. I cover each table with a linen tablecloth. In addition, I place a see through attractive and sturdy plastic tablecloth per table. When the party is over I dispose the plastic table cloths. The plastic tablecloth helps to keep the linen tablecloth clean and avoids a chocolate stained tablecloth. My experiences with chocolate fountains are very positive. They create excitement and much fun. There is something nostalgic about a chocolate fountain. People like to pick and choose the various items for dipping into chocolate. They also like the palette of food colors and decorations which make for a great dessert and a pleasing conversation. It is necessary to make this recipe for serving 25 to 50 people.

I find that I have best results with a chocolate fountain when using Ghirardelli® semi-sweet chocolate chips and Crisco® oil. The results are a smoother chocolate which is easier to work with when making this chocolate dessert. Do not use butter for it will separate the chocolate.

Pound cake can be substituted for the same amount of angel food cake.

Figure 3 cocktail napkins, 2-6 inch dessert plates and 8-10 frilled toothpicks per person. Encourage guests to take a clean toothpick for each item dipped into the chocolate fountain.

Frilled toothpicks can be purchased in boxes of 1000.

Chocolate Recipe for the Chocolate Fountain
Yield: 25-50 servings

5-12 ounce packages (each) Ghirardelli®
  semi-sweet chocolate chips
2 cups Crisco® vegetable oil

In top of a large double boiler, add the chocolate chips and oil. Stir until chocolate chips are melted and oil is blended. Turn on the chocolate fountain heater 15 minutes before serving. Pour the warm chocolate into the bottom of the chocolate fountain. (See illustration on page 148).

Chocolate Recipe for the Chocolate Fountain, continued

Suggested Dippers
Yield: 25 servings

2½ pounds fresh strawberries
5 large bananas
1 large fresh pineapple
¾ small angel food cake
1-1 pound box donut holes
1-10 ounce bag large marshmallows
1-12 ounce bag pretzels
200-250 frilled toothpicks
1 tray for used toothpicks
75 cocktail napkins
50 plastic 6 inch plates

Suggested Dippers
Yield: 50 servings

5 pounds fresh strawberries
10 large bananas
2 large fresh pineapples
1 small angel food cake
2-1 pound boxes (each) donut holes
2-10 ounce bags large marshmallows
2-12 ounce bags pretzels
400-500 frilled toothpicks
2 trays for used toothpicks
150 cocktail napkins
100 plastic 6 inch plates

Place the chocolate fountain on the covered table. Clean strawberries, leaving the hulls on each strawberry. Dry strawberries. Cut bananas into ¾-1 inch chunks. Dip chunks into lemon juice to prevent bananas from becoming brown. Dry off the bananas. Cut pineapple and angel food cake into bite size chunks. Arrange strawberries, bananas, pineapple and angel food cake chunks, donut holes, marshmallows and pretzels on tiered trays or clear bowls. Place the dippers on the chocolate fountain table. Place plates, napkins, frilled toothpicks and empty trays for used toothpicks Place the heated chocolate into the heated chocolate fountain. Turn on and let the chocolate flow like a champagne fountain. Listen to the guests' conversation about the chocolate fountain. Enjoy this special elegant dessert at your favorite bridal shower.

Chocolate Fountain Dessert

French Onion Soup
Soup á l'oignon
Yield: 24-one cup servings

6 tablespoons butter
2 tablespoons olive oil
3 pounds onions (thinly sliced)
4 quarts fat free beef stock
  (less 33% sodium)
1 teaspoon garlic powder
1 teaspoon dried thyme
¼ cup burgundy wine

In a heavy soup kettle, melt the butter with the olive oil over moderate heat. Stir in the onions and cook uncovered over low heat, stirring occasionally for 20 to 30 minutes, or until the onions are a rich golden brown. Sprinkle flour over the onions and cook, stirring for 2-3 minutes. Remove the kettle from the heat. In a separate pan bring the stock to a simmer and add the wine. Stir the beef stock-wine mixture into the onions. Continue to cook the soup over low heat and simmer partially covered for another 30 minutes. Serve with baguettes. (See photo below).

Guest Table Setup

Baguettes
Yield: 24 servings

2 loaves baguettes
1½ pounds Swiss cheese,
  shredded and divided

Slice bread into one inch thick slices. Place slices of baguettes on two cookie sheets. Place into oven and bake at 375F for 2-3 minutes on each side to toast the baguettes. Remove from the oven. Sprinkle 1 tablespoon grated cheese on top of each slice of baguettes. Ladle soup into oven proof soup bowls. Place one baguette slice on top of the soup. Return the soup bowls to the oven and continue to bake for 3 minutes or until cheese melts. Serve soup with extra baguette slices and your favorite crackers.

Pat's Favorite French Onion Soup
Yield: 20 servings

4 quarts beef stock
2 pounds onions,
  peeled and sliced
1 medium leek, chopped
2 tablespoons minced garlic
1 ounce fresh marjoram, chopped
1 teaspoon dried thyme
1 teaspoon freshly ground pepper
1-1 pound 3 ounce can chickpeas,
  drained and rinsed
¼ cup burgundy wine
20 slices whole wheat bread, toasted
1½ cups Swiss cheese

In a large stock pot, add the beef stock, onions, leek, garlic, marjoram, thyme, and pepper. Simmer over low heat for about 2 hours, stirring occasionally. Add wine and simmer for 10 more minutes. Stir in the chickpeas and cook for 5 more minutes. Follow the directions for making baguettes.

The Salade Nicoise

The Salade Nicoise is called the tuna, egg and tomato salad. This salad is healthy, colorful and easy to prepare. It requires almost no cooking. Serve this salad with fresh French bread for a delightful lunch. The name Salade Nicoise comes from Nice, a beautiful city on the Mediterranean Sea in the southern part of France. Many fish dishes are unique to this region. The ingredients are easy to exchange. Anchovies may be left out of the salad if so desired. (See photo below).

Tip

Suggested greens are red leafy lettuce, Boston lettuce, Romaine lettuce, endive and spinach. I never served the Salade Nicoise using fresh tuna for a very large group. I used canned tuna. The authentic Salade Nicoise is always served with fresh tuna. However, due to the cost, even restaurants in France are using canned tuna. Figure two servings per 6 ounce can when using canned tuna. Purchase a 4 pound 4 ounce can of tuna when serving a larger group.

Add 1 to 2 tablespoons lemon juice to the water to keep the color in the green beans during the cooking process. Whole frozen beans can be substituted for fresh green beans. Twenty four salads can be made up from a one pound bag of whole green beans, using six per salad.

The Salade Nicoise

Salade Nicoise
Yield: 12 salads

24 cups mixed greens, divided
3 pounds grilled tuna (48 strips),
    divided
24 small red potatoes, sliced, divided
72 fresh whole green beans, divided
3 teaspoons lemon juice
12 hard cooked eggs, divided
6 small tomatoes quartered wedges,
    divided
12 thinly sliced red onions, cut into
    ringlets, divided
72 large size pitted ripe olives, divided
36 anchovies rolled in capers, divided,
    optional

Salad Nicoise
Yield: 24 salads

48 cups mixed greens, divided
6 pounds grilled tuna (96 strips),
    divided
48 small red potatoes, sliced, divided
144 fresh whole green beans, divided
4 teaspoons lemon juice
24 hard cooked eggs, divided
12 small tomatoes quartered wedges,
    divided
24 thinly sliced red onions, cut into
    ringlets, divided
144 large size ripe olives, divided
72 anchovies rolled in capers, divided,
    optional

Line up 9-inch salad bowls into an assembly line. Place 2 cups of mixed greens into each salad bowl. Cut the cooked fresh tuna into strips (4 strips per salad). Boil the red potatoes and cook until fork tender. Drain off water, dry and slice or quarter each potato. Snip off the ends of green beans. Rinse green beans in cold water. Place green beans in a small amount of water with lemon juice. Bring to a boil and cook only until barely tender. Drain and rinse in cold water. Dry and set aside. Hard cook, peel and cut each egg into slices. Quarter tomatoes into wedges. Slice the red onions. Drain and dab dry ripe olives. Count out pitted ripe olives and anchovies. Arrange the tuna strips, potatoes, green beans, egg halves, quartered tomatoe wedges, sliced onion ringlets, ripe olives and anchovies onto each salad. Serve with creamy or French herb dressing.

Tip
If you do not want to use fresh herbs, substitute 1 teaspoon each of the dried oregano, basil, and thyme. I prefer using fresh herbs.

Salade Nicoise, continued

Oil and Vinegar Dressing Yield: 6 servings	Oil and Vinegar Dressing Yield: 12 servings	Oil and Vinegar Dressing Yield: 24 servings
1 cup olive oil	2 cups olive oil	4 cups olive oil
½ cup white wine vinegar	1 cup white wine vinegar	2 cups white wine vinegar
½ teaspoon basil	1½ teaspoons basil	2 teaspoons basil
½ teaspoon oregano	1½ teaspoons oregano	2 teaspoon oregano
½ teaspoon thyme	1½ teaspoons thyme	2 teaspoons thyme
2 green onions with tops	3 green onions with tops	4 green onions with tops
2 garlic cloves	3 garlic cloves	4 garlic cloves
2 tablespoons Dijon mustard	3 tablespoons Dijon mustard	4 tablespoons Dijon mustard
1 teaspoon cracked pepper	1½ teaspoon cracked pepper	2 teaspoons cracked pepper
½ teaspoon seasoned salt	¾ teaspoon seasoned salt	1 teaspoon seasoned salt

Method I

In a blender, add olive oil, vinegar, basil, thyme, oregano, green onions, garlic, Dijon mustard, cracked pepper and seasoned salt. Blend on high for 1 to 2 minutes until all the ingredients are blended together and are creamy. Serve with the Salade Nicoise.

Method II

Place olive oil, vinegar, basil, thyme, oregano, chopped green onions, crushed garlic, Dion mustard, cracked pepper and seasoned salt into a jar with a lid. Shake dressing until all ingredients are well blended. Serve with the Salade Nicoise.

The Story About My Neighbor

My neighbors live behind us, up on a hill. They are are worldwide travelers. One of their favorite countries is France. My neighbor lady always looks forward to ordering her favorite Salade Nicoise with fresh grilled tuna. As she describes her dining experience she has me salivating.

The Story About Chef Victor Seydoux

Chef Victor Seydoux was responsible for creating the chef salad at Hotel Buffalo in Buffalo, New York. Chef Seydoux studied in Switzerland, France and England. He landed his job at the Waldorf-Astoria Hotel and the Ritz Carlton in the United States. The kitchen manager ran a tight budget at the Ritz Carlton Hotel. He demanded that Chef Sydoux keep the cost down. He quietly put together the chef salad for some select customers. Other customers began requesting the salad. The restaurant put

Chef Salad

the salad on its' menu. Thus Victor Seydoux gave his salad the name Chef Salad. In Victor Seydoux time he generally served Thousand Island dressing while other chefs used bleu cheese and oil and vinegar. Today, many weight watchers request a dressing substitute of lemon wedges. (See photo above).

Tip

Details on the Traditional Chef Salad Ingredients

1-1 pound head romaine lettuce = 8 cups
1-9 ounce bag spinach = 8 cups
1-10 ounce bag shredded carrots = 3 cups or 12 servings
1 bunch green onions = 7 (may vary due to size of onion)
1 rib celery hearts = 2 tablespoons or 20 ribs per 1 pound package
1-10 ounce container grape tomatoes = 48
1 carton large eggs = 12
1 large cucumber = 30 slices
1 slice Swiss cheese = 1 ounce
1 slice cheddar cheese = 1 ounce
1 slice turkey = 1 ounce
1 slice ham = 1 ounce

There are 16 slices per pound of cheese and also meat. I also like to cut the center hard rib from the center of each romaine leaf.

The Traditional Chef Salad

Yield: 1 serving

1 cup romaine lettuce
1 cup spinach
¼ cup shredded carrots
1 green onion with top
2 tablespoons celery, chopped
6 grape tomatoes
1 hard cooked egg, sliced
3 cucumber slices
1 slice Swiss cheese, julienne
1 slice cheddar cheese, julienne
1 slice turkey, julienne
1 slice ham, julienne

In a 9 inch salad bowl, mix together the lettuce, spinach, carrots, onion and celery. Garnish with grape tomatoes, egg, cucumber slices, cheeses and meats. Serve with your favorite dressings.

Chart for Quantity for Making Chef Salads

Servings	6 servings	12 servings	18 servings	24 servings
Romaine lettuce	¾ pound	1½ pounds	2¼ pounds	3 pounds
	(6 cups)	(12 cups)	(18) cups	(24 cups)
Spinach	7¾ ounces	13½ ounces	1 pound	1 pound 11 ounces
	(6 cups)	(12 cups)	(18 cups)	(24 cups)
Shredded carrots	3 cups	6 cups	9 cups	12cups
Green onions	6 onions	12 onions	18 onions	24 onions
bunches needed	1 bunch	2 bunches	3 bunches	4 bunches
Celery hearts	6 ribs	12 ribs	18 ribs	24 ribs
(2 tablespoons per salad)				
Grape Tomatoes	¾ pint	1½ pints	2¼ pints	3 pints
Hard Cooked Eggs	6 eggs	12 eggs	18 eggs	24 eggs
Large Cucumber	$3/5$ of 1 cucumber 18 slices	$1\text{-}1/5$ of 2 cucumbers 36 slices	about 2 cucumbers 54 slices	about $2\text{-}2/5$ cucumbers 72 slices
Swiss Cheese	6 ounces	12 ounces	18 ounces	24 ounces
	6 slices	12 slices	18 slices	24 slices
Cheddar Cheese	6 ounces	12 ounces	18 ounces	24 ounces
	6 slices	12 slices	18 slices	24 slices
Turkey	6 ounces	12 ounces	18 ounces	24 ounces
	6 slices	12 slices	18 slices	24 slices
Ham	6 ounces	12 ounces	18 ounces	24 ounces
	6 slices	12 slices	18 slices	24 slices

Bottled Salad Dressing (Approximate Servings) for the Chef Salad

1-8 ounce bottle organic balsamic vinaigrette dressing serves 6
1-16 ounce bottle Thousand Island dressing serves 12
1 quart Ranch dressing serves 20
1 quart 8 ounces Vidalia onion vinaigrette dressing serves 24

Tip

Bleu cheese dressing tastes best when made 24 hours in advance. This dressing can also be used as a dip with fresh vegetables. It is especially tasty with cauliflower and carrots.

When bleu cheese dressing is made the day before, it will thin out. For a thicker dressing, reduce the milk to 6 tablespoons for 6 servings, ¾ cup for 12 servings, 1 cup for 18 servings and 1¾ cups for 24 servings. Increase Tabasco® sauce to taste if you prefer the dressing to have more zest.

Chart Sizes for Bleu Cheese Dressing

Servings	6 servings	12 servings	18 servings	24 servings
Blue cheese	½ cup	¾ cup	1 ⅔ cups	2 ½ cups
Light mayonnaise	½ cup	¾ cup	1 ⅔ cups	2 ½ cups
Light sour cream	½ cup	¾ cup	1 ⅔ cups	2½ cups
Fat free half and half	¼ cup	6 tablespoons	1¼ cups	1 ½ cups
Worcestershire sauce	1 teaspoon	2 teaspoons	3 teaspoon	4 teaspoons
Dehydrated garlic	½ teaspoon	1 teaspoon	2 teaspoons	3 teaspoons
Dehydrated onion	½ teaspoon	1 teaspoon	2 teaspoons	3 teaspoons
Tabasco® sauce	1 drop	2 drops	3 drops	4 drops

Mix together bleu cheese, mayonnaise, light sour cream, fat free half and half, Worcestershire sauce, garlic, onion and Tabasco® sauce. Place dressing into a serving bowl(s). Refrigerate until serving time. Serve with the chef salad.

French Pear Tart
Yield: 10 servings

Poaching Liquid

**3 fresh medium red pears,
 whole and peeled
4 cups water
1 cup sugar
1 tablespoon lemon juice**

Pastry (Pate Sucree)

**1-10 inch tart pan with loose
 bottom
6 tablespoons unsalted butter,
 softened
⅓ cup sugar
3 eggs
1 teaspoon almond extract
⅛ teaspoon salt
no-stick baking spray**

Frangipane
**1 cup almond slivers
6 tablespoons unsalted
 butter, softened
⅔ cup sugar
3 eggs
2 tablespoons flour
1 teaspoon almond extract
¼ teaspoon cinnamon
3 large fresh red pears, peeled,
 quartered, cut in halves, cored
 and sliced across**

French Pear Tart

French Pear Tart, continued

Glaze
1 cup apricot jam
1 tablespoon sugar
2 teaspoons almond extract or
1 tablespoon lemon juice
1 tablespoon flour
1 tablespoon unsalted butter

Garnish
Yield: 1 per pear tart slice

1 small scoop ice cream
1 tablespoon whipped cream
1 strawberry with stem
1 miniature French flag on
  a toothpick

To make the <u>poaching</u> liquid, combine the water, sugar, and lemon juice in a saucepan that is just large enough to hold the pears. Bring the liquid to a boil. Add the pears to the boiling liquid and reduce heat to a simmer. Poach the pears for about 15 minutes or until they are tender when pierced with a knife. Cool the pears to room temperature in the syrup.

To make the <u>pastry</u>, in a five quart mixer beat together, almonds, flour, butter, eggs, sugar, almond extract and salt until pastry forms a ball. Place the pastry in the refrigerator for one hour. Roll out the pastry on a lightly floured pastry board to fit the tart pan. Use no-stick baking spray to grease the tart pan. Line the tart pan with the pastry. Pierce the bottom crust with a fork. Line the top of the bottom crust with foil. Weight down the bottom crust with beans or pie weights. Bake at 375F for 8 minutes. Remove from the oven and remove the foil and the bean or pie weights. Bake for 4 more minutes.

To make the <u>frangipane</u>, beat together butter, sugar, eggs, almond extract, and cinnamon. Spoon the frangipane into the pastry. Reduce the heat to 350F. The frangipane should be full to the top of the crust. Core and thinly slice the pears. Place sliced pears evenly in a circle on top of the frangipane. Bake at 350F for 40-45 minutes. Cool 20 minutes. Remove the tart from the baking dish and place on a glass platter. Set aside.

French Pear Tart, continued

To make the <u>glaze</u>, in a saucepan mix together the jam, sugar almond extract or lemon juice, flour, and butter until smooth. Cook over low heat until jam melts and ingredients slightly thicken. Cool. Push the glaze through a sieve and brush on tart.

For the <u>garnish</u>, top each serving with one scoop of French vanilla ice cream, whipped cream, a fresh strawberry and a miniature French flag on a toothpick. (See photo on page 159).

Tip

Chocolate chips will burn if melted in a microwave for too long of a time. I prefer to use Ghirardelli chocolate chips when making the chocolate raspberry pear tart.

Chocolate Raspberry Pear Tart
Yield: 10 servings

Poaching Liquid

3 medium fresh red pears,
  whole and peeled
4 cups water
1 cup sugar
1 tablespoon lemon juice

Pastry (Pate Sucree)

1-10 inch tart pan with loose
  bottom
2 cups flour
6 tablespoons unsalted butter,
  softened
2 eggs
⅓ cup sugar
1 teaspoon almond extract
⅛ teaspoon salt
No-stick baking spray
1 cup pie weights or uncooked navy beans

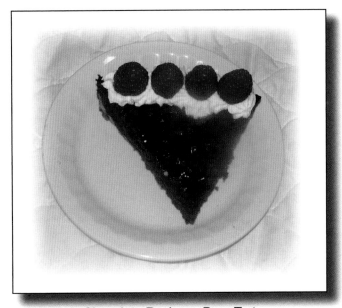

Chocolate Rasberry Pear Tart

Filling

1-12 ounce package
  Ghirardelli® chocolate chips
6 tablespoons unsalted butter, softened
4 ounces cream cheese, softened
  (½ of an 8 ounce package)
²/₃ cup sugar
2 eggs
1 teaspoon almond extract
1 cup slivered almonds, ground
⅓ cup flour
½ teaspoon cinnamon

Glaze

1 tablespoon flour
1 tablespoon butter
1 cup raspberry seedless jam
1 teaspoon almond extract
¼ teaspoon cinnamon, optional

Garnish

whipped cream, optional
1 quart French vanilla ice cream, optional
1 pint fresh raspberries, optional

To make the <u>poaching liquid</u>, combine the water, sugar, lemon juice in a saucepan, just large enough to hold the pears. Bring the liquid to a boil. Add the pears to the boiling liquid and reduce to a simmer. Poach the pears for about 15 minutes or until they are tender when pierced with a knife. Cool the pears to room temperature in the syrup.

To make the <u>pastry</u>, in a five quart mixer, beat together flour, butter, eggs, sugar almond extract and salt until pastry forms a ball. Place the pastry in the refrigerator for one hour. On a lightly floured board, roll out the pastry to fit the tart pan. Use no-stick baking spray to grease the bottom and sides of the tart pan. Line the tart pan with the pastry. Line the top of the bottom crust with foil.

Chocolate Raspberry Pear Tart, continued
Place the pie weights or beans over the foil. Bake at 375 for 6 minutes. Remove the pastry from the oven and remove the foil and pie or bean weights. Bake for 2 more minutes.

To make the frangipane, beat together the cream cheese, butter, sugar, eggs, almond extract and almonds. Melt the chocolate chips in top of a double boiler. Add the melted chocolate chips and flour to the batter. Beat together until smooth and creamy. Spoon the frangipane into the pastry. Core, quarter and thinly slice the pears into wedges. Place sliced pears evenly into two three circles on top of the frangipane and bake at 350F for 55-60 minutes.

To make the glaze, in a saucepan melt butter and whisk in the flour until smooth. Slowly whisk the jam into the flour-butter mixture to form a smooth glaze. Stir in the almond extract and cinnamon last. Remove from the heat. Cool. Brush glaze onto the tart. Cool thoroughly.

To garnish the tart, use number 30 cake tube, pipe on a border of fresh whipped cream. Decorate the border with fresh raspberries or serve with French vanilla ice cream and ready whipped topping with drizzled chocolate syrup and a French flag on a toothpick per serving. (See photo on page 161).

Tip

Most crêpe recipes say to make crêpe in a greased 8-10 inch skillet. I like to use a griddle to eliminate all the grease. I make sure the griddle is hot and I carefully turn over each crêpe with a thin metal spatula when the edges of each crêpe are dry.

The Mascarpone cheese filling is very tasty but cherry pie filling is also a crowd pleaser.

Chocolate Dessert Crêpes
Yield: 24-6 inch crêpes

4 cups milk
½ cup sugar
6 eggs
2 teaspoons chocolate
1 teaspoon almond extract
2 cups flour
¼ cup butter, melted
¼ teaspoon salt

Mix together the milk, sugar, eggs, chocolate flavoring and almond extract. Whisk in the flour a little at a time. Stir in the melted butter and salt to the crêpe batter. On a large griddle with temperature of 350F shape two 6 inch round crêpes by spreading ¼ cup crêpe batter each. Use the bottom of the measuring cup to spread the crêpe evenly into a circle. Loosen the bottom of the crêpe with a long stainless steel cake-decorating spatula. Flip the crêpe over with the pancake turner. Remove crêpes one at a time and place each one on an individual dinner plate. When cooled, place waxed paper in between each crêpe to prevent crêpe from sticking. Fill crêpe with various pie fillings or the Mascarpone cheese filling and roll into a diploma-like fashion. Serve with whipped cream, nuts or choice of chocolate chips or chocolate shavings.

Mascarpone Cheese Filling for Crêpes
Yield: 24 servings

1-8 ounce container Mascarpone cheese, softened
1-8 ounce package Neufchatel cheese, softened
1 cup seedless strawberry jam
½ teaspoon cinnamon
1 quart fresh strawberries
1 cup fresh blueberries

Beat together the Mascarpone and Neufchatel cheese until smooth and creamy. Add the strawberry jam, honey and cinnamon. Beat. Wash and dry the strawberries and blueberries. Slice the strawberries. Fold in the strawberries and blueberries. Serve with fresh whipping cream or non-dairy whipped topping.

Tip

The suggested dippers for the chocolate fondue are strawberries, pineapple, bananas, pound cake cubes, miniature donuts, pretzels and short bread cookies.

If you do not want to rent or own a chocolate fountain, the chocolate fondue idea is a great substitute and also great fun. Cut large plain donuts into 6 pieces per donut when substituting large donuts for miniature size ones. Large donuts are sold 12 to a package.

Chocolate Fondue	Chocolate Fondue	Chocolate Fondue
Yield: 6-8 servings	Yield: 12-16 servings	Yield: 24 servings
1-12 ounce package (each) chocolate chips	2-12 ounce packages (each) chocolate chips	3-12 ounce packages (each) chocolate chips
½ cup fat free half and half	⅔ cup fat free half and half	1 ⅓ cups fat free half and half
3 tablespoons kirsch or brewed hazelnut flavored coffee	5 tablespoons kirsch or brewed hazelnut flavored coffee	6 tablespoons kirsch or brewed hazelnut flavored coffee
¼ teaspoon cinnamon	½ teaspoon cinnamon	¾ teaspoon cinnamon

Heat chocolate and half and half in heavy saucepan over low heat, stirring constantly, until chocolate is melted and the mixture is smooth. Remove from the heat; stir in the kirsch liqueur or coffee. Pour into a fondue pot or chafing dish to keep warm.

Chart Listing for Ingredient Sizes for the Chocolate Fondue Dessert

Ingredients	Chocolate Fondue	Chocolate Fondue	Chocolate Fondue	Chocolate Fondue
Servings	Yield: 6 servings	Yield: 12 servings	Yield: 24 servings	Yield: 48 servings
Strawberries	1 pound strawberries	1 ¾ pounds strawberries	2 ½ pounds strawberries	5 pounds strawberries
1 large banana (8 one inch pieces)	2 large bananas	4 large bananas	5 or 6 large bananas	10 large bananas
Pound cake	½ of 16 ounce pound cake	1-16 ounce pound cake	1 ½-16 ounce pound cakes	2 -16 ounce (each) pound cakes
Miniature donuts (30 to a 13 ounce package)	½ of a 13 ounce package miniature donuts	1-13 ounce package miniature donuts	2 -13 ounce packages (each) miniature donuts	4-14 ounce packages (each) miniature donuts
Shortbread cookies (24 per 6 ounce box)	½ of a 6 ounce box shortbread cookies	1-6 ounce box shortbread cookies	2 -6 ounce boxes (each) shortbread cookies	4-6 ounce boxes (each) shortbread cookies
Pretzels (2 per person)	1-12 ounce package pretzels	2-12 ounce package pretzels	4-12 ounce package pretzels	1-30 ounce package pretzels

Follow instructions for the chocolate fountain layout of the dippers found on page 148.

For the entertainment or game part of the shower present a wedding word search to your guests. This can take place before or after the meal. Encourage the guests to divide up into groups of two or three's. The group that completes the word search first with all the correct answers gets the prize.

Wedding Word Search

```
ABGHIOPNIGGHHOOLMNBVFREWIUYTREDLKJJTUOPLMNBTFIANCEXCRTUIO
PROMANCEOPKJUYTGVFDEAMIJHYFDESWHUKONMIUYTGVFRTYUIKMJNBYG
FBBGYHJKILOPLKJHYTFRECBGTRESDFLOIKURINGBEARERRUIMJHTYULOVE
HHHGTTUUIOPLKJWEDDINGATTIREKLJHGVFRDXZAMBRIDEVOOMNOONKIM
HGRRENGAGEMENTKEEPRTPLOOKFTRSPOUSEFATEJAMNEEDFORTOOJUGTD
UGGYYHHIIMARRIAGEOOPPLKMJUHYGTFCDERHYFYIUYTFHONEYMOONDEE
DOONBONNIEDANNYDIAMONDRINGGIGHIMWEDDINGRECEPTIONCCDDYYIYA
GOTTBRIDESMAIDSTGYUJIKFDERLOPUYNGTRDZCTYHILMJUYGTFRCYHGFRU
OPKTYHYWEDDINGVOWSPPOMAIDOFHONORPOLKIMJUHYTTGBVFRRDEDOPK
TRFGHNBVFREDCXSWEDFTYHBRIDALSHOWERQWSXDZAETYUILPOIKMJUHBT
FLOWERGIRLNOPLKMNHYTFRESDRTYUKIJUHYTGGIFTOPENINGXERTIOJKGT
IGYOUIKLMNHYTGFRDFEMATRONOFHONORIOPLMNHYTGVFREDHYUIJHGTI
ZIPZAPHAPYAPLKIUJHYTGWEDDINGRINGSRPOLKIUJHYTGFCVFRTJHYTGFRE
DUMBERTYLOIKJUHYTGFRDESDRFGROOMNHGVCDEGARTERSOPLOKIJUHPP
WEDTIOPKJHYGTFREDHYJILOJHGTRDEWSDFRYUJIKWEDDINGDAYOPLKIUJH
YTTGYHUBRIDALBOUQUETOPKJUHYTGUESTSJUHYVRTYHUIONUIOKTFOPIHE
RFREDWSERYUIOKIJUHYTFRCELEBRATIONHUIKJNHEARTPLOKMNHYTFRDCA
NOPLKIJUHYGTRDVGTMKIJUHYGTFRDCOMMITMENTPLOKIJUHYGTFRDEWSC
```

Wedding Attire	Bridesmaids	Fiancé	Engagement
Wedding Rings	Maid of Honor	Flower Girl	Garter
Wedding Day	Matron of Honor	Bridal Bouquet	Marriage
Diamond Ring	Wedding Vows	Bridal Shower	Gift Opening
Wedding Reception	Bride	Spouse	Commitment
Ring Bearer	Groom	Honeymoon	Romance
Heart	Guests	Celebration	Love

Wedding Word Search Key

```
ABGHIOPNIGGHHOOLMNBVFREWIUYTREDLKJJTUOPLMNBT FIANCE XCRTUIO
P ROMANCE OPKJUYTGVFDEAMIJHYFDESWHUKONMIUYTGVFRTYUIKMJNBYG
FBBGYHJKILOPLKJHYTFRECBGTRESDFLOIKU RINGBEARER RUIMJHTYU LOVE
HHHGTTUUIOPLKJ WEDDINGATTIRE KLJHGVFRDXZAM BRIDE VOOMNOONKIM
HGRR ENGAGEMENT KEEPRTPLOOKFTR SPOUSE FATEJAMNEEDFORTOOJUGTD
UGGYYHHII MARRIAGE OOPPLKMJUHYGTFCDERHYFYIUYTF HONEYMOON DEE
DOONBONNIEDANNY DIAMONDRING GIGHIM WEDDINGRECEPTION CCDDYYIYA
GOTT BRIDESMAIDS TGYUJIKFDERLOPUYNGTRDZCTYHILMJUYGTFRCYHGFRU
OPKTYHY WEDDINGVOWS PPO MAIDOFHONOR POLKIMJUHYTTGBVFRRDEDOPK
TRFGHNBVFREDCXSWEDFTYH BRIDALSHOWER QWSXDZAETYUILPOIKMJUHBT
FLOWERGIRL NOPLKMNHYTFRESDRTYUKIJUHYTG GIFTOPENING XERTIOJKGT
IGYOUIKLMNHYTGFRDFE MATRON OF HONOR IOPLMNHYTGVFREDHYUIJHGTI
ZIPZAPHAPYAPLKIUJHYTG WEDDINGRINGS RPOLKIUJHYTGFCVFRTJHYTGFRE
DUMBERTYLOIKJUHYTGFRDESDRF GROOM NHGVCDE GARTER SOPLOKIJUHPP
WEDTIOPKJHYGTFREDHYJILOJHGTRDEWSDFRYUJIK WEDDINGDAY OPLKIUJH
YTTGYHU BRIDALBOUQUET OPKJUHYT GUESTS JUHYVRTYHUIONUIOKTFOPIHE
RFREDWSERYUIOKIJUHYTFR CELEBRATION HUIKJN HEART PLOKMNHYTFRDCA
NOPLKIJUHYGTRDVGTMKIJUHYGTFRD COMMITMENT PLOKIJUHYGTFRDEWSC
```

Wedding Attire	Bridesmaids	Fiancé	Engagement
Wedding Rings	Maid of Honor	Flower Girl	Garter
Wedding Day	Matron of Honor	Bridal Bouquet	Marriage
Diamond Ring	Wedding Vows	Bridal Shower	Gift Opening
Wedding Reception	Bride	Spouse	Commitment
Ring Bearer	Groom	Honeymoon	Romance
Heart	Guests	Celebration	Love

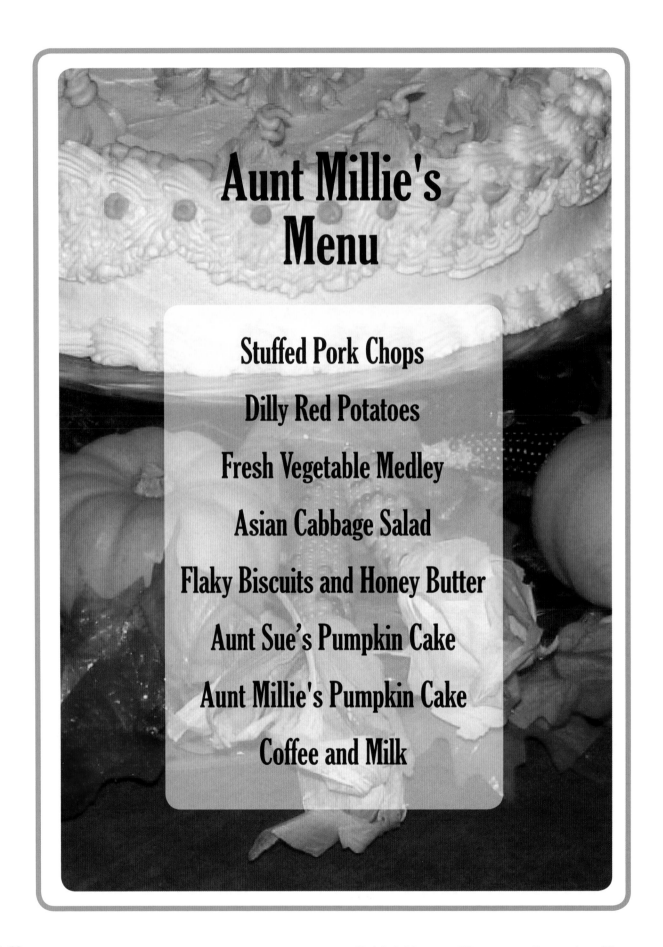

Aunt Millie's Menu

Stuffed Pork Chops

Dilly Red Potatoes

Fresh Vegetable Medley

Asian Cabbage Salad

Flaky Biscuits and Honey Butter

Aunt Sue's Pumpkin Cake

Aunt Millie's Pumpkin Cake

Coffee and Milk

Chapter 8
Fallen in Love Bridal Shower Theme

A Love Story

Eric attended University of Wisconsin Milwaukee and majored in civil engineering. He always enjoyed any food with pumpkin and his favorite desserts are pumpkin cake and pumpkin pie.

Eric was very busy on a blustery fall morning and decided to head over to the school cafeteria after his last class. He got into line and immediately spotted the last piece of his favorite pumpkin cake. There was a tiny and attractive young lady in front of him. She too had her eye on the same piece of pumpkin cake. When she reached out to pick up the cake, he immediately said, "Wait, this is my piece of pumpkin cake. Okay!" She replied, "I am sorry, but I was here first. It is my piece of pumpkin cake. "Okay!" He sighed. Eric then said, "I have a great idea." He would buy the cake and split it with her. She agreed. He paid for the cake and asked for an extra plate, fork and knife. He cut the cake in half and offered to sit with her while sharing the cake. He did not ask her name nor did she volunteer her name. She ate her cake and went on her own way. A couple weeks went by, and he saw her again at a Halloween party. He spoke to her and thought that it was strange to see her again. She did not tell him her name, and he did not ask. Finally, he met her again at a Campus Crusade meeting, and this time he finally asked her name. As they continued to meet at the Campus Crusade meeting, they became better acquainted and finally, after a year of dating, it was very obvious that they were falling in love. Eric and Heather were always together. He introduced her to my husband and me at a dinner, and we were thrilled that he had a wonderful girlfriend.

On his birthday, he proposed to Heather. She thought that they were going out for his birthday but little did she know that she was about to become engaged.

Eric is an only child and Heather is from a family of seven. Heather's sisters reserved a hall at an Irish pub and held a shower in November.

All of the family and friends received invitations that said "Surprise." Cousin, Pat volunteered to make their wedding cake for a gift, and made arrangements to meet Heather at lunch the Monday before the shower to firm up details for the wedding cake. During lunch Heather asked, "Are you coming to my bridal shower?"I immediately asked, "What shower?" She replied, "I know that there is a shower for me. I just don't know where." I swallowed hard. I let her know that I was not going to say anything and I quickly changed the subject.

On the day of her shower, her sister picked her up for the noon luncheon bridal shower and blindfolded her so she could not see where they were going. Finally, when they arrived, everyone yelled "Surprise!" Heather confessed that she knew that there was a shower planned for her, but she did not know where.

Her best friend's aunt made a pumpkin cake decorated with calla lilies. The cake elicited a lot of conversation. Heather's dear friend acted as hostess at the bridal shower. She had each person stand up, introduce herself and explain how she knew Heather. I joked about trying to remember every person's name at each table. I did remember all the guests at my table and enjoyed the visit with Heather's family. We ordered lunch from a selected menu of a variety of salads and sandwiches. No prices were listed because the family wanted to treat us for coming.

They also hired Irish dancers in for the entertainment. The youngest dancer had blond hair and big blue eyes and stole the show. After the show, the guests played a couple of games.

One of the games involve Heather's name. We were given a piece of blank paper and a pen. We were instructed to write down words found within Heather's name. The one that had the most words from Heather's name won the prize. Only five minutes were allowed for this game.

Game Using Heather's Name

1. Eat	6. Hare	11. Rat	16. Heath	21. Tee	26. Hear
2. Heat	7. Heart	12. He	17. Tar	22. Heater	27. Rhea
3. Ate	8. Ear	13. Tea	18. Tear	23. Era	28. The
4. Rate	9. Here	14. A	19. Hat	24. Ether	29. Thee
5. There	10. Her	15. At	20. The	25. Rate	30. Three

The winner had 18 correct words. One of the ladies at the shower thought she was to make up words only from Heather's first initial (H). I was sitting next to her as she went gang busters and wrote the words down by using the letter "H." When she realized her mistake, she was a good sport and all laughed with her.

Another game played at the shower was interesting to me. Before the shower Eric had to answer 15 questions about Heather. The hostess read the questions out loud one by one, and Heather had to answer each question to see if her answer would match Eric's. For every wrong answer, Heather had to chew a stick of gum. She ended up with six sticks of gum. The guests cheered Heather on to blow a big bubble. It was great fun watching her face and listening to her comments. She enjoyed the game as much as the guests.

Lunch ended with a delicious pumpkin cake. Heather then opened her presents and was especially excited that her bridal party had chipped in to purchase her a red Kitchen Aide mixer. Heather thanked everyone for coming to her shower. She was very gracious and thanked us for our good wishes upon her upcoming wedding day. The guests continued to visit with Heather and family.

After the shower Aunt Millie wanted to do something special for the happy couple. She decided to have a sit down dinner so people could get better acquainted with

Aunt Millie's Guest Table Setup

Eric and Heather. Aunt Millie always has the right set of dishes for just about every occasion. She thought that it would be fun for the guests to learn how Eric and Heather met at school. She would serve pumpkin cake for dessert. She would use her pumpkin dishes and decorate her entire table with a pumpkin and fall theme.

She set her table with a gold tablecloth, silverware, plates with a pumpkin border, pumpkin salad dishes and dessert plates. She also used her leaf adorned napkin rings. She used her green colored glasses for beverages. She adorned the center of the table with a fall centerpiece of pumpkins and miniature colored corns on a glass plate and placed it on a riser. The fall napkin covered the riser and matched the guests napkins. Two candles decorated with leaves in the candle holder were on each side of the centerpiece. She used coffee mugs for coffee. (See photo on page 171).

Aunt Millie decided to make two different styles of pumpkin cake for the guests and have the guests vote on their favorite style cake. Aunt Sue volunteered to give her recipe to Aunt Millie for the shower. Aunt Sue had entered her pumpkin cake in two contests and won 1st prize in both contests. Aunt Millie had her grandmother's old-fashion pumpkin cake recipe.

There were several guests who did not know each other. Aunt Millie decided a game to have strangers interact was in order. She gathered leaves from the trees in her back yard. She made name tags using the leaves and asked the guests to find a matching leaf and learn something about that person.

Leaf Name Tags

Select two leaves of each variety that look alike to make a total of your guests. Dry leaves thoroughly. Spray each leaf with extra-hold hair spray. Place each leaf on waxed paper and dry. Place a second piece of waxed paper on top of each leave. Place books over the waxed paper to keep the leaves flat. Place the name of each guest on a label. Place label in the middle of each leaf. Run a stick pin through the top of a leaf. Place all the leaf name tags on a small table near the entryway of your home or party area. When guests arrive, instruct each guest to find the guest with the same matching leaf and become acquainted with the guest.

Aunt Millie wanted the meal to be simple and filling, but also elegant. She decided on the perfect menu which can be found on page 168. She would serve coffee with the cake after the meal. She had enough space and table settings for 20 people. Usually she stuffed her own pork chops, but if she lacked time the butcher shop would accomplish the job.

Tip

Each ½ pound pork chop is filled with ⅓ cup of stuffing. One cup of stuffing fills three pork chops. The crock pot stuffing recipe fills 42 half pound pork chops. Three pounds of stuffing stuffed 18 pork chops. For every three pork chops, melt one tablespoon of butter. Use 2 teaspoons Italian bread crumbs for each pork chop. Use ½ teaspoon granulated garlic per tablespoon of melted butter. Use 2 teaspoon granulated garlic per 6 tablespoons of melted butter. Remember less is more when cooking with spices in quantity.

Chart for Pan Size and Baking Time for Stuffed Pork Chops

Pan Size	Baking Time
8x8 pan holds 4-½ pound pork chops	Bake at 375F uncovered for 1 hour.
9x13 pans holds 8-½ pound pork chops	Bake at 375F uncovered for 1hour.
Chafing dish insert pan 12x20x½inch deep holds 16-½ pound pork chops	Bake at 375F uncovered for 1 hour and 10 minutes or until meat is no longer pink.

Chart for Vegetable Broth Used Pan Size for Baking Pork Chops	Chart for Amount of Marsala Wine in Pork Chops
½ cup vegetable broth per 8x8 pan	¼ cup Marsala wine per 8x8pan
1 cup vegetable broth per 9x13 pan	⅓ cup Marsala wine per 9x13 pan
1⅔ cups vegetable broth per 12x20x 2½ inch deep chafing dish insert pan	½ cup Marsala wine per 12x20x½ inch deep chafing dish insert pan

Stuffed Pork Chops
Yield: 20 pork chops

20-½ pound (each) butterflied pork chops
6²/₃ cups stuffing, divided (¹/₃cup
  per pork chop)
6 tablespoons plus 2 teaspoons
  butter, melted and divided
2 teaspoons granulated garlic
¾ cup plus 1 tablespoon and 1 teaspoon
  Italian bread crumbs, divided
3¼ pounds stuffing, divided
2-14 ounce cans (each) 100% fat
  free vegetable broth
1 cup plus 2 tablespoons Marsela wine

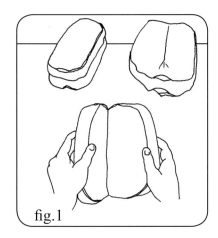
fig.1

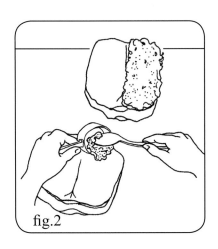
fig.2

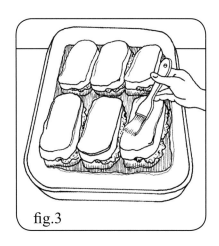
fig.3

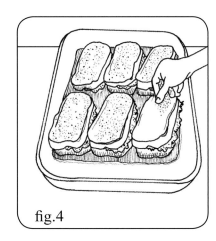
fig.4

Wash pork chops and dab dry. Open butterflied left half pork chop (fig.1) and place ¹/₃ cup stuffing on the right half of each pork chop. Fold the top of the pork chop over the stuffing to sandwich the stuffing between the two layers of each pork chop (fig.2). Follow the chart for vegetable broth and Marsela wine for each appropriate size pan on page 173. Mix together the broth and wine. Pour into the bottom of each pan. Mix together the butter and garlic. Brush the garlic butter mixture over the top of each pork chop (fig. 3). Sprinkle 2 teaspoons of bread crumbs over each pork chop (fig. 4). Bake pork chops, uncovered at 375F for 1 hour to 1 hour and 10 minutes or no longer pink with an internal temperature of 160-170F. Refer to details for pan size and baking time on page 173.

The stuffing recipe is not low in calories but so yummy and easy to make ahead of time for any special occasion. Two 7½ ounce packages of Martha White® yellow Cornbread mix is used in Southern stuffing recipes. However, it is not easy to find the cornbread mix in the North. Substitute this particular brand with white or yellow cornmeal.

Crock Pot Stuffing
Yield: stuffing for 42 half pound
            butterflied pork chops

3 cups cornmeal
1-16 ounce package of Pepperidge Farm®
 seasoned stuffing mix (7 cups)
3 cups unseasoned cubed
 wheat and white stuffing
1-10 ¾ ounce can cream of celery soup
1-10 ¾ ounce can cream of mushroom soup
1-10 ¾ ounce can cream of chicken soup
1-14 ounce cans 99% fat free chicken broth
½ cup no-fat evaporated milk
1 medium onion, chopped
1 tablespoon minced garlic
1½ cups chopped celery and leaves
½ cup (1 stick) butter, melted
2 teaspoons poultry seasoning
½ teaspoon salt
1 teaspoon cracked pepper
no-stick baking spray

Mix together cornmeal, stuffing mixes, cream of mushroom soup, cream of celery soup, cream of chicken soup, chicken broth, evaporated milk, onion, garlic, celery, butter, eggs, poultry seasoning, and salt and pepper until all the ingredients are blended. Spray the large crock pot with no-stick baking spray. Spoon the dressing into the crock pot. Cover and cook on low for 3 hours. If the stuffing becomes dry, add an extra ⅓-½ cup chicken stock and thoroughly stir into the stuffing.

Fresh Steamed Vegetable Medley, continued

1 teaspoon dried thyme
3 tablespoons olive oil
1 cup shredded cheddar cheese
  divided

2 teaspoons dried thyme
5 tablespoons olive oil
2 cups shredded cheddar cheese,
  divided

Fresh Steamed Vegetable Medley
Yield: 40 servings

3 pounds fresh broccoli flowerets
3 pounds fresh cauliflower flowerets
2 pounds fresh baby carrots
1½ red bell pepper, diced
1½ yellow bell peppers, diced
5 small zucchini, sliced
1½ medium red onions,
  sliced in ringlets
2-8 ounce packages (each) sliced
  mushrooms
2 tablespoons minced garlic
2 teaspoons cracked pepper
5 teaspoons Mrs. Dash® tomato basil
  seasoning
1 tablespoon dried thyme
½ cup olive oil
3 cups shredded cheese

Fresh Steamed Vegetable Medley
Yield: 50 servings

4 pounds fresh broccoli flowerets
4 pounds fresh cauliflower flowerets
3 pounds fresh baby carrots
2 red bell peppers, diced
2 yellow bell peppers, diced
6 small zucchini, sliced
2 medium red onions,
  sliced in ringlets
2½-8 ounce packages (each) sliced
  mushrooms
2½ tablespoons minced garlic
1 tablespoon cracked pepper
6 teaspoons Mrs. Dash® tomato basil
  seasoning
4 teaspoons dried thyme
¾ cup olive oil
3¼ cups shredded cheese

Rinse broccoli, cauliflower and baby carrots. Take core out of cauliflower. Add the carrots. Clean and remove the core from the peppers. Dice peppers. Add peppers, zucchini, onion ringlets, mushrooms and garlic to the vegetable medley. Place 1 quart water into the bottom of a vegetable steamer pan for each batch. Place vegetables into a large bowl. Add the Mrs. Dash® tomato basil seasoning, thyme and olive oil. Place the vegetables into the top of the vegetable steamer. Place the top of the steamer pan over the bottom of the steamer pan. Cover and steam vegetables until barely tender or 3-6 minutes. Place cooked vegetables in an appropriate sized greased pan(s) and sprinkle cheese over each pan of vegetables. Cover with foil and bake for 5 minutes or until cheese melts. See chart on page 177 for the amount of vegetables to fit into the top of a steamer.

Asian Cabbage Salad Setup

Asian Cabbage Salad
Yield: 10 servings

1-2 pound head red cabbage
1-8 ounce can sliced water chestnuts, drained
2 tablespoon Hormel® Real Bacon pieces
½ cup celery, diced
½ cup Craisins®
2 green onions with tops, chopped
¼ cup red onion, diced
1½ teaspoons minced garlic
⅓ cup dry roasted sunflower kernels
⅓ cup sliced almonds
2-3 ounce packages (each) Ramen® noodles, crushed (discard flavor packets)

Asian Cabbage Salad
Yield: 20 servings

1-3 pound head red cabbage
1-8 ounce can sliced water chestnuts, drained
1-2.28 ounce jar Hormel® Real Bacon pieces
1 cup celery, diced
1 cup Craisins®
4 green onions with tops, chopped
½ cup red onion, diced
1 tablespoon minced garlic
⅔ cup dry roasted sunflower kernels
⅔ cups sliced almonds
3-3 ounce packages (each) Ramen® noodles, crushed (discard flavor packets)

Asian Cabbage Salad
Yield: 40 servings

2-3 pound heads (each) red cabbage
2-8 ounce cans (each) sliced water
  chestnuts, drained
2-2.8 ounce jars (each) Hormel®
  Real Bacon Bits
1¾ cups celery, diced
1¾ cups Craisins®
2-15 ounce cans (each) Mandarin
  oranges, drained
6 green onions with tops, chopped
¾ cup red onion, diced
2 tablespoons minced garlic
1½ cups dry roasted sunflower kernels
1 cup sliced almonds
5-3 ounce packages (each) Ramen®
  noodles, crushed (discard flavor
  packets)

Asian Cabbage Salad
Yield: 50 servings

7 pounds red cabbage
2- 8 ounce cans (each) sliced water
  chestnuts, drained
3-3.8 jars (each) Hormel®
  Real Bacon Bits
2 cups celery, diced
2 cups Craisins®
3-15 ounce cans (each) Mandarin
  oranges, drained
8 green onions with tops, chopped
1 cup red onion, diced
3 tablespoons minced garlic
2 cups dry roasted sunflower kernels
1¼ cups sliced almonds
7-3 ounce packages (each) Ramen®
  noodles, crushed (discard flavor
  packets)

Tip
Good Seasons® Italian salad dressing is sold in a box of four 0.7 packets and also sold individually in 0.7 packets. Ramen® noodles become soft if mixed into the salad a day before.

Asian Salad Dressing
Yield: 10 servings

½ cup white balsamic vinegar
¾ cup olive oil
1-0.7 ounce package Good Season®
  Italian dressing mix
1 tablespoon honey
2 teaspoons Splenda®
2 tablespoons lite soy sauce
1 teaspoon 5 spice seasoning

Asian Salad Dressing
Yield: 20 servings

1 cup white balsamic vinegar
1¼ cups olive oil
2-0.7 packages (each) Good Seasons®
  Italian dressing mix
2 tablespoons honey
3 teaspoons Splenda®
3 tablespoons lite soy sauce
2 teaspoons 5 spice seasoning

Asian Cabbage Salad, continued

Asian Salad Dressing
Yield: 40 servings

1¾ cups white balsamic vinegar
2¼ cups olive oil
5-0.7 packages (each) Good Seasons®
  Italian dressing mix
4 tablespoons honey
5 teaspoons Splenda®
5 tablespoons lite soy sauce
3 teaspoons 5 spice seasoning

Asian Salad Dressing
Yield: 50 servings

2½ cups white balsamic vinegar
2¾ cups olive oil
6-0.7 packages (each) Good Seasons®
  Italian dressing mix
6 tablespoons honey
6 teaspoons Splenda®
6 tablespoons lite soy sauce
4 teaspoon 5 spice seasoning

Clean the cabbage and chop into bite size pieces. Place cabbage in a large bowl. Add the water chestnuts, bacon pieces, celery, craisins, Mandarin oranges, green onions, red onion, minced garlic, sunflower kernels and almonds. Set aside. In a medium size bowl, whisk together vinegar, olive oil, Good Seasons® Italian dressing mix, honey, Splenda®, soy sauce and 5 spice seasoning. Stir dressing into the salad and toss until well coated. Refrigerate the salad. Place Ramen® noodles in a gallon size storage bag. Close the bag. With a rolling pin, crush the Ramen® noodles. On the day of the party, mix in the Ramen® noodles into the salad. (See photo on page 179).

Tip

There are 20 leaves in a head of leafy lettuce weighing three- fourth pound. Green Leafy lettuce often has fewer leaves in a one pound head due to the size of each leaf.

Leafy Lettuce Chart

Yield: 10	**Yield: 20**	**Yield: 40**	**Yield: 50**
½ head leaf lettuce	1 head leaf lettuce	2 heads leaf lettuce	2½ heads leaf lettuce

Tip

There are 40 Mandarin oranges in a 15 ounce can. Use four mandarin oranges to garnish each individual salad.

The chart below includes only the number of Mandarin oranges for the garnish. See recipe for the amount used in the Asian cabbage salad with portions of 10-50 on page 179-180.

Chart for Mandarin Oranges

Number of Salads	Number of Mandarin oranges	Number of 15 ounce cans Mandarin oranges
10 salads	40	1 can
20 salads	80	2 cans
40 salads	160	4 cans
50 salads	200	5 cans

Tip

There are 40 green pepper strips to a large green pepper.

Green Pepper Garnish

Number of Salads	Number of Green Pepper Strips per salad
1 salad	2 green pepper strips
10 salads	20 green pepper strips
20 salads	40 green pepper strips
40 salads	80 green pepper strips
50 salads	100 green pepper strips

Assembling the Asian Cabbage Salad for a Sit-Down Dinner

Cut off the core from the leaf lettuce. Clean and dry each leaf. Place one leaf per pumpkin salad or salad bowl. Drain the Mandarin oranges. Pat the orange sections dry with paper towel. Remove the core from each bell pepper. Cut green peppers into strips. Set aside. Place approximately 1 cup of salad onto each plate, dividing the salad among 20 plates. Place 2 green pepper strips that crisscross to make an X in the middle of each salad and place 4 Mandarin oranges on all four sides of the X. Refrigerate the salads until serving time. (See photo on page 183). To save time and extra work, use a salad and biscuit station to create a semi sit down dinner.

Asian Cabbage Salad   Biscuit Basket with Bowls of Honey

Tip

Aunt Millie made the best biscuits but she decided to purchase the flaky biscuits in a can to save time. There are eight biscuits per can. A 13x17 baking sheet pan fits 12 biscuits. Catering services bake 24 biscuits per 17x25 baking sheet pan.

Biscuit Detail

Chart for Number of Biscuits for the Following Number of Guests

Flakey Biscuits Yield: 10 guests	**Flakey Biscuits Yield: 20 guests**	**Flakey Biscuits Yield: 40 guests**	**Flakey Biscuits Yield: 50 guests**
2-16.3 ounce cans (each) extra jumbo biscuits with flakey layers 16 biscuits	4-16.3 ounce cans (each) extra jumbo biscuits with flakey layers 32 biscuits	6-16.3 ounce cans (each) extra jumbo biscuits with flakey layers 48 biscuits	7-16 ounce cans (each) extra jumbo biscuits with flakey layers 56 biscuits

Preheat oven to 350 F. Place biscuits 1 inch apart on ungreased baking sheet(s). Bake 15-18 minutes or until golden brown. Serve warm with honey butter.

Tip

Place one stick of butter on each guest table and also one dish of honey butter.

Chart for Making Honey Butter

Yield: 10 servings	Yield: 20 servings	Yield: 40 servings	Yield: 50 servings
1 cup butter	2 cups butter	4 cups butter	5 cups butter
⅓ cup honey	⅔ cup honey	1 cup honey	1⅓ cups honey
1 teaspoon cinnamon	1½ teaspoons cinnamon	2 teaspoons cinnamon	2½ teaspoons cinnamon

Soften butter. Beat together butter, honey and cinnamon, (do not overbeat). Divide honey butter into 1 cup glass bowls and place one per table of 8 guests. Using a number 1C large star cake tip, pipe on star flower decorations on each of the 1 cup honey butter. (See biscuit basket with bowls of honey butters on page 183).

Aunt Sue's Pumpkin Cake
Yield: 10 servings

1 cup canola oil
2 cups sugar
4 eggs, separated
¼ cup hot water
1¾ cups (15-ounce can) pureed pumpkin
1 teaspoon vanilla
2½ cups sifted flour
1 tablespoon baking powder
¼ teaspoon salt
1 tablespoon pumpkin pie spice
½ cup chopped toasted pecans
1 cup golden raisins

Preheat oven to 350F. Grease 3 nine-inch round cake pans. Line bottoms with parchment paper. Lightly grease parchment paper. Combine oil, sugar, egg yolks and water in mixer bowl. Beat at medium speed just until combined. Stir in pumpkin and vanilla. In a separate bowl, whisk together flour, baking powder, pumpkin pie spice and salt. Add to pumpkin mixture and mix just until moistened. Stir in raisins and pecans. Beat egg whites until stiff. Fold in batter. Spoon batter evenly into prepared pans. Bake at 350F for 20 to 25 minutes or until toothpick inserted in the center comes out clean. Remove cakes from oven and cool on wire racks for 5 minutes. Remove from pans; remove parchment paper and cool layers completely (bottom sides down) on wire racks before assembling. Refrigerate finished cake.

Aunt Sue's Orange Whipped Cream Cheese Frosting
Yield: Frosting for 1 pumpkin cake

2-8 ounce packages (each) cream cheese, softened
4 tablespoons butter, softened
1 cup heavy whipping cream, chilled
1 cup plus 2 tablespoons powdered sugar
1½ teaspoons unflavored gelatin softened over 2 tablespoons water
1½ tablespoons frozen orange juice concentrate, thawed
1 teaspoon vanilla
½ teaspoon crème bouquet
a few drops of orange food coloring, optional

In a 5-quart mixing bowl, cream together butter and cream cheese. Add 1 cup sifted powdered sugar, vanilla, orange juice concentrate, crème bouquet and food coloring. Beat well and set aside. Heat unflavored gelatin mixture in microwave for 10 seconds to dissolve gelatin. Cool slightly. In medium chilled bowl and using chilled beaters, beat whipping cream at medium speed until frothy. Add remaining 2 tablespoons powdered sugar, sifted, and dissolved gelatin mixture. Continue beating until stiff peaks form. Fold whipped cream mixture into the cream cheese mixture. Use to fill and frost cake.

Tip
The orange whipped cream cheese frosting holds up well enough to pipe on rosettes around top and bottom edge of the cake.

Aunt Millie's Pumpkin Cake
Yields: 10 servings

2 cups sugar
1 cup canola oil
4 large eggs
2 cups flour
2 teaspoons baking soda
1 teaspoon baking powder
½ teaspoon salt
1 teaspoon cinnamon
2 teaspoons pumpkin pie spice
2 cups pumpkin puree

Aunt Millie's Pumpkin Cake

Combine sugar, canola oil and eggs in a large mixing bowl; mix well. Sift dry ingredients into a separate bowl; stir into oil mixture, beating well. Stir in pumpkin puree. Pour batter into three greased and floured 9-inch round layer cake pans. Bake at 350F for 20-25 minutes or until toothpick inserted in the center comes out clean. Place cakes on cooling racks for 5 minutes. Turn cakes out onto racks to cool. Frost the pumpkin cake with cream cheese frosting.

Aunt Millie's Cream Cheese Frosting
Yield: frosting for 3- 9 inch round cakes

¼ cup butter
1-8 ounce package cream cheese, softened
1 pound powdered sugar, sifted
2 teaspoons vanilla

Beat together butter and cream cheese. Add powdered sugar a little at a time to the butter mixture. Add the vanilla and beat frosting until smooth and creamy.

Tip

Aunt Millie used the cream cheese frosting between the layers and the butter cream frosting for the outside of the cake and also decorating the cake.

Butter Cream Frosting
Yield: 1 whole 9-inch cake

1 cup shortening
1 cup butter, softened
1-2 pound package
  powdered sugar
⅓ cup water
½ teaspoon salt
1 teaspoon vanilla
4 drops orange food coloring
3 drops green food coloring

Beat together shortening and butter until smooth and creamy. Slowly add the powdered sugar to the shortening/butter mixture alternating with the water. Add the salt and vanilla and continue to beat until the frosting is smooth and creamy. Frost the bottom and second layer of cake with Aunt Millie's cream cheese frosting. Frost the outside of the cake with the butter cream frosting. Dip cake spatula into warm water to smooth the frosting on the cake. Using 2 bowls, place approximately 1 cup of frosting and orange food coloring in one bowl and ¾ cup of and green food coloring in the second bowl. Mix food coloring thoroughly through each bowl of frosting. Set aside. Using a three-inch round cookie cutter, outline a half circle all the way around the side of the cake. Using a number 30 star cake tip, pipe on the outline of each half circle. Fill in the half circles with frosting stars. With the same tip pipe on top and bottom borders. Using a number 1C large star cake tip, pipe on 10 orange pumpkins 1½ inches apart on top of the cake inside of the border. Place a three-inch round or pumpkin cookie cutter in the center of the cake to make an outline. Continue piping on 4 pumpkins around the outline and an x in the middle of the circle. Using a number 5 writing tip, pipe on green stems on all 14 pumpkins and connect each pumpkin with a green squiggly line. Pipe on green dots on the side of the cake at the bottom of the border. Refrigerate the cake until serving time.

How to Display Aunt Millie's and Aunt Sue's Pumpkin Cakes

2 lengths of silk fall leaves
9 miniature pumpkins
12 miniature colored
  corns with corn stalks
1 large platter, inverted
1 round riser or 2 inch
  round dish

Pumpkin Cakes Setup

Place large platter in a selected area for display of the pumpkin cake. Place the riser in the middle of the platter. Place Aunt Sue's cake on the riser and Aunt Millie's cake off to the side of Aunt Sue's cake. Place the silk leaves around the bottom of the cake plate. Aternate 6 miniature pumpkins with 6 two colored corns with silk leaves around the bottom of the cake. Place pumpkin dessert plates next to the cake. (See photo on page 185 and above).

A Berry Beary Christmas Menu

Christmas Pomegranate
Cranberry Punch
Puff Pastry Appetizers
Salsa
Mushroom Soup
Holiday Salad
Stuffed Salmon
Brown and Wild Rice Pilaf
Berry Acorn Squash
Multi Wheat Rolls
Cranberry muffins
Butter Roses
Heart Sugar Cookies
Lemon Sherbet
Coffee and Milk

Chapter 9
A Berry Beary Christmas Bridal Shower Theme
A Casual Beary Christmas Bridal Shower Theme

Story

Roxanne and Chad grew up together in the same neighborhood. They were playmates. Chad was always very protective of Roxanne and also very close to her family, especially to her father, Harold. Roxanne suspected the reason Chad held a special place in her dad's heart had to do with a story about her father that her grandmother told her. Harold had been a Boy Scout leader and wanted a son very badly. When Roxanne's mother became pregnant, Harold wrote her a beautiful letter expressing his love, happiness and excitement about the birth of their first child. A baby boy was born, but unfortunately he was premature and lived only 19 hours. Roxanne's mom was pregnant again one year after her brother's death. When this baby arrived the nurse informed Harold that he had a very healthy baby girl, Harold said, "A girl—I want a boy. It must be a mistake." According to Roxanne's grandmother, the nurse gave Harold a tongue lashing that he would never forget. Roxanne came to understand that Chad helped fill a part of that empty place in her dad's heart that had been left there with the death of his first-born son.

Roxanne also knew how much her dad loved her and saw him show it in so many ways. Normally, Chad and Roxanne would walk to school together, but one day Chad was sick and Roxanne started off by herself. Harold surprised Roxanne as he caught up with her and offered to walk to school with her. Roxanne protested that she was "a big girl" and could walk to school by herself. Harold, hurt by this rejection, (as Roxanne's grandmother later told her), nevertheless, lagged behind her as she completed her first solo walk to school. Roxanne, in spite of her boasts of being old enough to walk by herself, secretly took comfort in knowing that her dad was close behind.

Throughout their childhood, Chad and Roxanne shared many wonderful times with Roxanne's dad. Three times a week during their summer vacation from school, Harold would come home from work and pack Roxanne, Chad and the other neighbor kids into his shiny red Chevy and take them to Eagle Lake to swim. After swimming, they were told to dry off for the next stop was at the local ice cream parlour for ice cream cones. The kids all enjoyed Harold's jokes and dry sense of humor and even put up with his off-key singing.

One day while Chad and Harold were playing ball in the street, Chad challenged Harold to a race. While running after Chad, Harold fell, broke his wrist and ended up in the hospital. Chad felt terrible and so responsible, but Harold assured him the injury was not his fault. The incident seemed to bind them even closer.

Chad and Roxanne shared the same birthday and for their 5th birthday, Roxanne's grandmother made them each an identical teddy bear. They took their bears to school for show-and-tell. Years later, Roxanne still had her teddy bear and kept him on her bed. Roxanne learned from Chad's mother that Chad still had his teddy bear, which he kept on his dresser top.

Roxanne always felt Chad was a good person with a loving heart. They had been so connected during their childhood with shared memories of Roxanne's father and his influence on them and with all the neighborhood kids. However, it bothered her terribly that, as they reached the dating years, Chad was a good 5 inches shorter than Roxanne. Eventually they drifted apart and went their separate ways.

At age 24, Roxanne was back in her hometown and began teaching at the local high school. She loved her work and her students. Chad was a pilot in the Air Force, fulfilling a life-long passion for airplanes. He looked very impressive in his Air Force blues and had no trouble finding dates, but somehow the relationships never seemed quite right. He called Roxanne and told her he would be coming home in a month on leave. Wouldn't it be great to get together for old-time's sake and catch up on each other's lives? Roxanne let him know she too had been thinking of him.

After his leave was up, Chad promised to stay in touch. He was going to be out of the Air Force in a year and intended to find a job close to home. He missed everyone. Roxanne found herself thinking of Chad more and more as that year went by. He was so kind and thoughtful of her. They had so much in common. Roxanne was older now and more mature. She realized the difference in their heights made no difference at all. After Chad moved back home, they continued to date and fell in love. In October, Chad spoke to Harold and asked for his daughter's hand in marriage. Roxanne's father was delighted. A week later, Chad arrived at Roxanne's with his teddy bear. He and the bear got down on bended knee and he told Roxanne that she was the love of his life and asked her to marry him. Of course, she accepted. A childhood friendship had turned into true love and a longing to spend the rest of their lives together.

Aunt Marta's Bear Decoration Ideas for the Bridal Shower

Roxanne's Aunt Marta thought it would be great fun to have a wedding shower for the couple at Christmas time. She remembered their identical teddy bears and learned that they each still had (and treasured) the bears. Of course, the shower would have a Christmas theme and Aunt Marta decided to also incorporate the bears. She could outfit them as a bride and a groom.

Aunt Marta's Thoughts about the Bridal Shower Party Setup

Aunt Marta has a 13 foot buffet in her newly remolded spacious dining room. She thought it was a good idea to have the guests start off the fun by milling around and helping themselves to punch and puff pastry appetizers. She would use her Christmas dishes for the entire meal and serve the dinner in courses. She would set up the buffet for the punch and appetizer course and display the bride and groom teddy bears with accents of berries and mini Christmas trees made from ice cream cones decorated with royal icing, décor red hots and miniature red gummy bears. She would carry out the bear theme throughout the shower. Also, since she had the time she would make sure every guest received a decorated Christmas tree to remember the shower.

Christmas Pomegranate Cranberry Punch Setup

Tip

An average size punch cup holds a little over a half cup. Figure 2 servings of punch per person. Know the capacity of the punch bowl for your party. If a punch bowl holds 3½ quarts fill the punch bowl with 3 quarts of punch and leave space for the ice mold and fruit. Also measure the size of the ice mold to be sure that it will fit into the punch bowl. Aunt Marta generally uses a star mold for her Christmas parties. Her star mold is 4 inches wide and 3 inches deep and holds 1 quart of liquid. She always uses 7-UP® in the ice mold. Water dilutes the punch. Freeze the 7-UP® in the ice mold 24 hours before the party. Unmold the frozen 7-UP® star in advance and place it into a bag and return to the freezer until serving time. Aunt Marta's punch bowl is 12 inches across the top and tapers in toward the bottom. She combines the punch ingredients about 15 minutes before the guests arrive.

Christmas Pomegranate Cranberry Punch
Yield: 4 quarts

1 quart orange juice
1 quart pomegranate cranberry juice
2 quarts 7-UP®, divided

Garnish
1 large orange or 2 limes, sliced

Pour 1 quart 7-UP® into the star mold. Freeze for 24 hours. On the day of the party, in a large punch bowl, add orange juice, pomegranate cranberry juice and 1 quart 7-UP®. Gently stir together the ingredients. Remove the ice mold from the freezer bag and gently place the mold into the punch bowl. Slice an orange or limes and garnish the punch by placing the lime or orange slices around the outer sides of the 7-UP® mold. (See illustration on page 197).

Puff Pastry Pinwheel Appetizers	Puff Pastry Pinwheel Appetizers
Yield: 20 puff pastry appetizers	Yield: 40 puff pastry appetizers
1 puff pastry sheet	2 puff pastry sheets
¼ cup butter, melted	½ cup butter, melted
1 teaspoon granulated garlic	2 teaspoons granulated garlic
¼ cup sour cream	½ cup sour cream
¼ cup medium salsa	½ cup medium salsa

Puff Pastry Pinwheel Appetizers, continued

2 tablespoons egg, beaten	1 egg, beaten
½ cup four cheese Mexican cheese	1 cup four cheese Mexican cheese, divided
½ teaspoon cumin	1 teaspoon cumin
½ cup fresh cilantro leaves, chopped	1 cup fresh cilantro leaves, chopped
salsa	salsa

Thaw puff pastry in the refrigerator. Lightly dust the pastry board or counter top with flour. Place one puff pastry sheet on the board. Melt butter and add the granulated garlic to the butter. Set aside. Mix together sour cream, salsa, and egg according to the number of puff pastries needed. Add cumin and cilantro leaves and stir thoroughly. Brush each puff pastry sheet lightly with the garlic butter. Spread the sour

Puff Pastry Pinwheels

cream mixture equally over each puff pastry sheet and sprinkle ½ cup of cheese on each puff pastry sheet. Starting at the end, roll up the puff pastry sheet like a diploma. Cut each roll into 20 pinwheels. Place each pinwheel onto a cookie sheet lined with parchment paper. Bake at 400F for 15 minutes or until golden brown. Place onto serving tray(s) and serve warm with salsa. (See illustration above).

How to Set Up the Punch and Appetizer Buffet, Using a 6-Foot Table From Left to Right for Buffet Setup

1. Cocktail napkins
2. Glass plates
3. Salsa
4. Puff pastry appetizers
5. Place garland (6 feet) or to fit the length of a table.
6. On the garland, alternate 5 heart candy canes with a single candy cane.
7. Place the 5 Christmas bulbs between the heart candy canes on the garland.
8. Place Christmas trees into groups of two or three along the inside and outside of the garland.

Setting the Table for the Sit-Down Dinner and Soup Setup

1. Cover table with red tablecloth liner.
2. Place the red liner with a lace tablecloth.
3. Place one charger plate at each place setting.
4. Place Christmas plate liner on charger.
5. Place 1 soup bowl on plate liner per guest.
6. Place soup tureen and ladle on soup tureen plate in the center of the table.

One Place Setting per Person

1. Salad fork
2. Dinner fork
3. Knife (with blade toward plate)
4. Spoon
5. Soup spoon
6. Water glasses (at the tip of the knife)
7. Rolled napkin in Christmas napkin ring
8. Place soup tureen and ladle on soup tureen plate in the center of the table.

Decorations on the Guest Table

1. Place six small pine tree branches and six clumps of berries around tureen.
2. Alternate silver and green Christmas bulbs with clumps of red berries.
3. Place a candle holder with Christmas candles on each side of the soup tureen.
4. Fill each bowl of soup and garnish with parsley and one heart shaped red bell pepper per guest.

Holiday Christmas Tree Salad Details
Yield: 12 Christmas Trees

1-5 ounce box sugar ice cream cones (12 per box)

Royal Icing
Yield: 12 Christmas trees

3 tablespoons meringue powder
4 cups sifted confectioner's sugar
7 tablespoons water
green food coloring
12-4 inch glass round plates

Holiday Christmas Tree Salad Details, continued

Decorations for Christmas Trees
Yield: 12 Christmas trees

24 gummy bears (2 per tree)
1-2 ounce Cake Mate®
  cinnamon red hot decors
6 tablespoons confectioner's
  sugar, divided

Place meringue powder, 4 cups confectioner's sugar. Add 7 tablespoons of water one tablespoon at a time, while beating until smooth. Add a couple drops green food coloring and beat until the food coloring is evenly distributed throughout the royal icing. Using a pastry bag and a 352 leaf tip, pipe on straight lines around the circumference of each tree from top to bottom. Starting at the top of the tree to make leaves to cover the entire body of the ice

Holiday Christmas Tree Salad with Red Wine Salad Dressing

cream cone. Using a small sifter, sift confectioner's sugar over the top and sides of each tree. Pipe on a small amount of frosting on the top of each tree. With a tweezers, randomly place the cinnamon decors around the Christmas tree. Place two gummy bears on the top both front and back. Place each tree on a 4-inch glass plate and let dry. Each tree will harden as it dries. Place each plated edible tree onto the center of a salad plate.

Information on Salad Ingredients for the Christmas Tree Salad

1 seedless cucumber yields 46-50 slices.
1 tomato yields 4-5 slices
1 bunch red leafy lettuce yields 10 salads.
Shredded carrots are sold in 10-ounce packages.

Amount of Ingredients Used for One Christmas Salad

4 cucumber slices
2 slices tomato slices, cut in half
4 avocado wedges
2 leaves of red leafy lettuce

Christmas Tree Salad	Christmas Tree Salad
Yield: 6 salads	Yield: 12 salads
2 tomatoes, sliced thin	4 tomatoes, sliced thin
24 cucumber slices	48 cucumber slices
2 large ripe avocadoes, peeled and cut into wedges	4 large avocadoes, peeled and cut into wedges
½ cup shredded carrots	1 cup shredded carrots
6-4 inch plates	12-4 inch plates
6 decorated Christmas trees, divided	12 decorated Christmas trees, divided

Cut each tomato in half. Set aside. Slice cucumbers and set aside. Clean and chop lettuce. Dab dry with paper towel. Place each 4 inch plate with Christmas tree onto the center of a 9 inch salad plate. Place lettuce around each 4 inch glass plate with Christmas tree. For each salad, use 4 cucumber slices, 4 tomato half slices, 4 avocado wedges and 2 leaves of red leafy lettuce. Alternate tomatoes, cucumber slices and avocado wedges around the outer edge of each salad plate. Garnish with three small bundles of shredded carrots in between the tomatoes and cucumber slices. (See illustration on page 203).

Tip

Organic balsamic vinaigrette comes in a 32-ounce bottle. This dressing can also be served with the Christmas tree salad. There are many raspberry vinaigrette dressings on the market. The Walden Farms® has an exceptional raspberry vinaigrette dressing that is calorie free, sugar free, carbohydrate free, gluten free and cholesterol free. It comes in a 12-ounce bottle. Walden Farms®, Inc. is based in Linden NJ 07036. On page 203 is a delicious homemade red wine dressing which complements the Christmas tree salad.

Red Wine Salad Dressing
Yield: 6 servings

¼ cup mayonnaise
2 tablespoons olive oil
½ teaspoon Worcestershire sauce
½ cup red wine vinegar
1 teaspoon basil
1 teaspoon minced garlic
½ teaspoon Splenda®
½ teaspoon white pepper

Red Wine Salad Dressing
Yield: 12 servings

½ cup mayonnaise
¼ cup olive oil
1 teaspoon Worcestershire sauce
1 cup red wine vinegar
2 teaspoons basil
2 teaspoons minced garlic
1 teaspoon Splenda®
1 teaspoon white pepper

In a blender, add mayonnaise, olive oil, Worcestershire sauce, vinegar, garlic, Splenda® and pepper. Blend ingredients until smooth and creamy. Serve in a small to medium size glass bowl with a soup serving spoon.

Tip

One 48 ounce package frozen salmon contains 8-12 individually wrapped salmon pieces depending on the size of each piece. Each serving of salmon is filled with ⅓ cup spinach/feta cheese filling. Fresh cooked spinach cooks up to less than half. For example, a 13-ounce package of fresh spinach will yield ½ cup when cooked whereas a 10 ounce package frozen spinach yield ¾ cup. It is also time consuming to cut off the tails of each spinach leaf. Frozen chopped spinach is already cooked, but it is necessary to thaw and squeeze out the excess liquid. Using frozen spinach helps save preparation and cooking time.

One 13x9 pan holds 9 servings of salmon and a 12x20x4 inch deep steam pan holds 24 servings.

Stuffed Salmon
Yield: 6 servings

6 frozen salmon fillets, thawed
3 teaspoons lemon juice, divided
2-13 ounce packages (each) fresh
 baby spinach
½ cup feta cheese
1 egg
1 teaspoon dehydrated minced onion

Stuffed Salmon
Yield: 12 servings

12 frozen salmon fillets, thawed
2 tablespoons lemon juice, divided
3-13 ounce packages (each) fresh
 baby spinach
1 cup feta cheese
2 eggs
2 teaspoons dehydrated minced onion

1 teaspoon salmon seafood seasoning	2 teaspoons salmon seafood seasoning
1 teaspoon dried dill weed	2 teaspoons dried dill weed
1 teaspoon Worcestershire sauce	2 teaspoons Worcestershire sauce
1 teaspoon minced garlic	2 teaspoons minced garlic
2 tablespoons melted butter, divided	¼ cup melted butter, divided
4 tablespoons Italian bread crumbs, divided	8 tablespoons Italian bread crumbs, divided
1 cup vegetable broth	2 cups vegetable broth
⅓ cup white cooking wine	⅔ cup white cooking wine

Stuffed Salmon
Yield: 18 servings

18 frozen salmon fillets, thawed
3 tablespoons lemon juice, divided
4-13 ounce packages (each) fresh
 baby spinach
3 eggs
1½ cups feta cheese, crumbled
3 teaspoons dehydrated minced onion
3 teaspoons salmon seafood seasoning
1 tablespoon dill weed
2½ teaspoons Worcestershire sauce
3 teaspoons minced garlic
6 tablespoons melted butter, divided
¾ cup Italian bread crumbs, divided
3 cups vegetable broth
1 cup white cooking wine

Stuffed Salmon
Yield: 24 servings

24 frozen salmon fillets, thawed
4 tablespoons lemon juice, divided
5-13 ounce packages (each) fresh
 baby spinach
4 eggs
2 cups feta cheese, crumbled
4 teaspoons dehydrated minced onion
4 teaspoons salmon seafood seasoning
4 teaspoons dill weed
1 tablespoon Worcestershire sauce
4 teaspoons minced garlic
½ cup melted butter, divided
1 cup Italian bread crumbs, divided
4 cups vegetable broth
1⅓ cups white cooking wine

Thaw salmon in the refrigerator for 24 hours before preparation time. Rinse off salmon in cold water and pat dry. Slice each piece of salmon lengthwise through the center leaving a hinge at the opposite end. Brush the top of each piece with lemon juice (½ teaspoon per salmon). Cut off the tails of each piece of spinach. Rinse thoroughly. Place spinach and water into a stock pot and bring to a boil for about 4-5 minutes or until spinach is tender and cooked through. Drain the spinach and squeeze out the excess water. Chop the spinach. Set aside. In an appropriate size bowl, mix together the spinach, feta cheese, egg(s), onion, salmon seafood seasoning, dill weed, Worcestershire sauce and minced garlic.

Stuffed Salmon, continued

Cover one half of each butterflied salmon with ⅓ cup of the spinach/feta cheese filling. Bring the other half of salmon over on top of filling. Mix the vegetable broth and wine together. Place vegetable broth and wine mixture into the bottom of appropriate size pan(s). Brush the top of each piece of salmon with the melted butter. Evenly sprinkle 2 teaspoons of bread crumbs over the top of each piece of salmon. Place salmon into the bottom of the baking pan(s) with the bread crumb side up. Bake at 400F, uncovered, for 20-25 minutes or until the internal temperature is 160 degrees.

Tip

Aunt Marta usually adds 1 cup cooked wild rice per 4 cups cooked brown rice. Aunt Marta always serves each guest ½ cup of cooked rice. For best results when cooking rice, add 2½ cups water to 1 cup raw rice. For softer and more tender rice, increase cooking time. One cup raw brown rice makes 2 cups cooked rice and 4 ounces of uncooked wild rice makes 1 cup cooked rice. There are 5½ cups of rice to a 32 ounce bag of brown rice. For six guests, use three cups cooked rice pilaf, with ½ cup portions. Rice pilaf can be made a day ahead of time and refrigerated and re-heated on the day of the party or made a week in advance, frozen in air tight bags and reheated on the day of the party.

Tip

Some directions on the back of a box or package of rice calls for 1 cup raw rice to 2½ cups water, salt and olive oil . For best results, follow the package or box directions. Bring water to a boil and add the brown rice. Reduce the heat and simmer for 35-45 minutes or until tender. Do not increase the amount of salt for larger batches of rice. A little salt goes a long way.

Chart for Red Bell Pepper Heart Detail for Garnishing Brown Rice

½ red bell pepper	16 aspic hearts
1 red bell pepper	32 aspic hearts
1½ red bell peppers	48 aspic hearts
2 red bell peppers	64 aspic hearts
2½ red bell peppers	80 aspic hearts
3 red bell peppers	96 aspic hearts
3½ red bell peppers	112 aspic hearts

Brown Rice, continued

Chart for Various Sizes of Ingredients Used in Brown Rice

1-10 ounce bag shredded carrots	3 cups
1-16 ounce bag frozen peas	3 cups
1 pound 12 ounce bag frozen peas	5 cups
1 pound butter	4 sticks butter (½ cup each stick or 1 pound)
1-4½ ounce jar minced garlic	4 tablespoons
1-48 ounce jar minced garlic	6 cups
1-15ounce can chicken stock	approximately 2 cups
1-3 pound 1-ounce can chicken stock	6 cups

Chart for Amounts of Cooked Rice Per Serving at a Glance

Uncooked Brown Rice	Water	Olive oil	Salt	Yield: number of ½ cup servings of cooked rice
1 cup	2½ cups	1 tablespoon	¼ teaspoon	2 cups (4½ cups)
2 cups	5 cups	5 teaspoons	½ teaspoon	4 cups (8-½ cups)
3 cups	7 cups	2 tablespoons	¾ teaspoon	8 cups (16-½ cups)
4 cups	2 quarts	3 tablespoons	1 teaspoon	11 cups (22-½ cups)
7 cups	3 quarts + 2 cups	6 tablespoons	1¼ teaspoon	19 cups (38-½ cups)
8 cups	4 quarts	7 tablespoons	1½ teaspoons	21 cups (42-½ cups)
9 cups	4 quarts + 2 cups	8 tablespoons	1¾ teaspoons	23 cups (46-½ cups)
10 cups	4 quarts + 3 cups	9 tablespoons	2 teaspoons	25 cups (50-½ cups)

Directions for Cooking Brown Rice
Add the salt and olive oil to the water. Bring to a boil. Add the rice. Turn the heat down to low. Cover the rice and simmer 45-60 minutes or until rice is tender.

Chart for Wild Rice   Chart for Wild Rice

Yield: 3 servings	Yield: 24 servings
2½ cups water	8 cups water
1 tablespoon olive oil	3 tablespoons olive oil
¼ teaspoon salt	1 teaspoon salt
1 cup rice	4 cups rice

Directions for Cooking Wild Rice
In an appropriate size pan, add olive oil and salt to the water. Bring to a boil. Add wild rice, cover pan and reduce heat to low. Simmer for about 60 minutes. For firmer rice, decrease cooking time.

The brown and wild rice pilaf chart explains the amounts needed for the various size servings. The first column of the chart lists the ingredients used in making cooked rice pilaf. The second column shows the amounts of ingredients. The second column also gives the amount of 16 aspic red bell pepper hearts needed for the cooked rice pilaf. The third column lists 5 red bell pepper hearts for garnishes or a total of 21 aspic hearts.

The third column also lists 6-½ cup servings cooked rice pilaf. The fourth, fifth and sixth columns repeat the ingredients, amounts and yield to make 14-½ cup servings cooked rice pilaf. There are 32 aspic hearts in the rice pilaf and 14 for garnishes or a total of 46. See charts below for details of ingredients, amounts and yield. Apply the same knowledge to the brown and wild rice pilaf chart II as to the brown and wild rice pilaf Chart I.

Chart for Ingredient Measurements for Brown and Wild Rice Pilaf I

Ingredients	Amounts	Yield:	Ingredients	Amounts	Yield:
Butter	2 tablespoons	6-½ cup	Butter	¼ cup	14-½ cups
Brown rice	2 cups cooked	servings	Brown rice	4 cups cooked	servings
Wild rice	¼ cup cooked	cooked rice	Wild rice	½ cup	cooked rice
Chicken stock	¼ cup	pilaf	Chicken stock	½ cup	pilaf
Frozen peas	⅓ cup		Frozen peas	½ cup	
Shredded fresh carrots	4 teaspoons		Shredded fresh carrots	3 tablespoons	
Red bell pepper	16 aspic hearts	5 for garnish	Red bell pepper	32 aspic hearts	14 for garnish
Minced garlic	½ teaspoon		Minced garlic	1 teaspoon	
White pepper	¼ teaspoon		White pepper	½ teaspoon	
Onion powder	¼ teaspoon		Onion powder	½ teaspoon	

Chart for Ingredient Measurements for Brown and Wild Rice Pilaf II

Ingredients	Amounts	Yield:	Ingredients	Amounts	Yield:
Butter	½ cup	22-½ cups	Butter	¾ cup	30-½ cups
Brown rice	8 cups		Brown rice	11 cups	
Wild rice	¾ cup		Wild rice	1¼ cups	
Chicken stock	1 cup		Chicken stock	1½ cups	
Frozen peas	1½ cups		Frozen peas	2 cups	
Shredded fresh carrots	¼ cup		Shredded fresh carrots	⅓ cup	
Red bell pepper	64 aspic hearts	22 for garnish	Red bell pepper	80 aspic hearts	30 for garnish
Minced garlic	2 teaspoons		Minced garlic		
White pepper	¾ teaspoon		White pepper		
Onion powder	¾ teaspoon		Onion powder		

Brown Rice, continued

Cut each red bell pepper in half and take out the core. Using an aspic cutter, cut out the hearts for each serving of rice pilaf. In an appropriate size pan for amount of ingredients, melt butter over low heat. Add the cooked brown rice, wild rice, chicken stock, peas, carrots, red bell pepper hearts, minced garlic, white pepper and onion powder. Stir ingredients thoroughly and simmer until ingredients are heated through. Serve the rice pilaf as part of the main course for dinner.

Tip
Aunt Marta blanched each squash whole, using one or more pans for the number of squash needed. She cut each squash in half, cleaned out the seeds and lined up each half on the countertop. She also lined up all the ingredients in an assembly line and filled each cavity. A 13x9 pan holds 6 squash halves. A 12x20 x 4 inch deep steam pan holds 12-15 squash halves depending on the size. Try to use small squash for best results.

Berry Acorn Squash
Yield: mixture for 1 serving

½ of a whole acorn squash
⅛ teaspoon salt
⅛ teaspoon white pepper
⅛ teaspoon granulated garlic
2 teaspoons brown sugar
1 tablespoon butter, melted
1 tablespoon amaretto liqueur
6 Craisins®, per serving
2 teaspoons finely chopped
  pecans

Berry Acorn Squash
Yield: mixture for 6 servings

3 whole acorn squash, cut in half
¾ teaspoon salt, divided
¾ teaspoon white pepper, divided
¾ teaspoon granulated garlic, divided
4 tablespoons brown sugar, divided
6 tablespoons, butter, melted, divided
6 tablespoons amaretto liqueur, divided
36 Craisins®, divided
4 tablespoons finely chopped
  pecans, divided

Fill a large stock pot with water. Bring the water to a boil. Add each whole acorn squash to the water and blanch the skins of each squash for 3-5 minutes. Remove the squash and cool. With a sharp chef knife, cut each acorn squash in half. Crosswise, cut a thin slice off the bottom of each acorn squash to help the squash lay flat in the baking pan. Remove seeds and strings. Place squash cut side up in a baking pan filled with ¼ inch water. Following the recipe above, fill each squash half with salt, pepper, granulated garlic, brown sugar, butter, amaretto liqueur, Craisins® and pecans. Gently stir ingredients in each squash cavity. Cover squash

Berry Acorn Squash, continued

with foil and bake at 375F for 35-40 minutes or until the flesh of the squash is tender. (See illustration on page 216).

Tip

Millet is any of several small grained cereal grasses. Rolls can be made a day before the shower. Store rolls in the refrigerator and reheat in the microwave for 15 seconds. Place rolls in a basket with lined green napkin. Place on the guest table with salads or pass the rolls.

Multi Grain Rolls
Yield: 24 Rolls

1-3 pound package of 24 frozen
 bake and serve multi-grain rolls
 with sunflower seeds and millet
2 muffin tins (12 per pan)

Grease each muffin cup with no-stick baking spray. Place one roll per muffin cup. Spray the top of each roll with no-stick baking spray. Cover rolls with plastic and cover the plastic with a towel. Place rolls in a warm area such as on top of the stove or turn on the oven and preheat the oven to 350F. Turn the oven off. After the temperature comes down to warm, place the rolls in the oven and let the rolls rise until double in size (about 4 hours). Remove the rolls from the oven and preheat the oven to 350F. Bake the rolls for 10-14 minutes or until golden brown. Remove the rolls from the muffin pan at once and place rolls on a wire rack to cool. (See illustration on page 212).

Tip

Aunt Marta liked to make 2 batches of 30 each when making cranberry muffins. She usually lined up all the ingredients and used two bowls, placing like ingredients in each bowl in an assembly line-fashion. She also mixed the muffins by hand to barely moisten the dry ingredients to avoid tunnels in the baked muffins. She froze the baked muffins, 6 to a package. The cranberry muffins can be made 3 days ahead of the party. She preferred to use fresh cranberries when in season.

**1-5.25 ounce jar Wilton®
  pearlized sugar sprinkles
36 red cinnamon gummy bears**

Preheat the oven to 350F. Cream butter and sugar together. Add eggs, vanilla and almond extract; beat. Add flour to the mixture, a little at a time, and continue to beat until dough is blended together. Add a couple drops of red food coloring to the dough to make a rose color and beat until food coloring is blended well. Sprinkle flour on work surface. Roll out the dough to about ⅛-¼ inch thick. Using a 4 inch wide heart cookie cutter, cut out the hearts. Place hearts on the cookie sheet lined with parchment paper. Sprinkle each cookie with the pearlized sugar. Bake for about 10-12 minutes or lightly golden on the bottom of the cookie. Make a batch of royal icing (page 203). Place a small dab of royal icing on the back of each gummy bear and stick the bear onto the center of each cookie.

Tip

There are approximately 30-32 raspberries in a half pint, 4 servings sherbet per pint, and approximately 32 mint leaves in a ⅔ ounce package of mint. Freeze the lemon flowerets to act as an ice base to keep the sherbet from melting.

Lemon Sherbet	Lemon Sherbet
Yield: 8 servings	**Yield: 16 servings**
4 fresh lemons	**8 fresh lemons**
2-1 pint containers (each) lemon sherbet	**4-1 pint containers (each) lemon sherbet**
16 fresh mint leaves	**32 fresh mint leaves**
8 white 5½ inch (each) heart shaped doilies, divided	**16 white 5½ inch(each) heart shaped doilies, divided**
16 heart shaped cookies (2 per person)	**32 heart shaped cookies (2 per person)**

Cut V's into the center of each lemon, going all the way around the lemon and pull apart the lemon to form 2 flower halves. Freeze the lemons overnight. On the day of the party (in a footed sherbet glass), place one frozen lemon flower and top with one scoop of lemon sherbet. Place one raspberry and 1 sprig of mint leaves onto each party pick. Place pick into the top of each scoop of lemon sherbet. For each guest, place the filled sherbet glass onto a 7-inch plate lined

Lemon Sherbet, continued

with a 5½-inch white heart doily. Place 2 heart shaped cookies decorated with a gummy bear garnish on each dessert plate. (See illustration below).

Tip
Lemon sorbet is used for cleansing the pallet for a dinner served in courses. Sorbet is time consuming, to make but well received at a sit down dinner. It takes only 20 minutes to make, but it takes a day to complete sorbet. While Aunt Marta did not make sorbet, she thought it would be good to include it in the recipe.

Lemon Sorbet
Yield: 6 servings

Peel from 1 lemon, finely diced
1 cup water
½ cup sugar
½ cup lemon juice
½ cup carbonated mineral water
6 strips lemon zest for garnish

In a sauce pan, stir together the diced lemon peel, 1 cup water and sugar. Bring the mixture to a boil and reduce to medium heat. Simmer for 5 minutes to make

Lemon Sherbet and Heart Sugar Cookies
with Bear Garnish

syrup. Remove from the heat and allow the mixture to cool. In a bowl, stir together the lemon syrup with peel, lemon juice and mineral water. Pour into an ice cream maker or a tall canister and freeze for about 1½ hours. Remove from the freezer and stir with a whisk. Return to the freezer. Stir every hour for a total of 4 hours. A lemon sorbet is a lighter product if stirred frequently. Garnish each serving with a twist of lemon peel.

Coffee and Milk Detail

Refer to the Fallen in Love in Fall Bridal Shower Chapter on page 188 for coffee and milk details.

There are 18 medium pieces to a bunch of flowering kale which weighs ½ pound. Aunt Marta used the flowering kale and one slice of blood red orange as a garnish on each dinner plate. One blood red orange yields 5 slices depending on the thickness of each slice. There are 60 green grapes to a medium bunch. Three green grapes will fill a 2¼ inch party pick.

How to Assemble Each Dinner Plate

1 stuffed salmon
½ acorn squash
½ cup rice pilaf
1 flowering kale leaf
1 slice of fresh blood orange
3 green grapes on a party pick

Place salmon on the plate with the rice to the left of salmon. Place the squash to the right of the salmon and the orange/grape garnish to the right of the rice pilaf.

One Guest's Plated Food

The Truth Game
Give each guest a chance to tell other guests at their table two statements that are true and one false thing.

Example I
I hate to cook
I won the prize in my class for reading the most books.
I love my wife's good cooking

Example II
I enjoy watching sports
I am good at water skiing
I am a citizen of U.S.

The Answer Game

The responses are numbered 1-12. Maybe, You Hope, Whatever, You Bet, Unsure, Crazy About You, Very Funny, Sometimes, Absolutely, Wishing, Never, I'm Thinking

Type up the answer list below.

1. Maybe
2. You Hope
3. Whatever,
4. You Bet
5. Unsure
6. Crazy About You
7. Very Funny
8. Sometimes
9. Absolutely
10. Wishing
11. Never
12. I'm Thinking

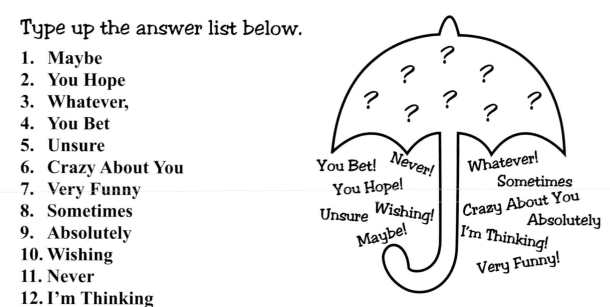

We are going to play the answer game. Previous to the shower make up one list per guest with answers numbered 1-12. Fold list in half so as to hide the answers from view. To play the game, explain that there will be a questioner and an answerer. The questioner will ask the person on his right a question. (See examples below.) The person on the right responds with a number from 1-12. The questioner unfolds his list and reads off that numbered response. The game continues with each guest and can generate some very funny answers.

Examples

Do you like to swim? (Maybe)
Do you like to eat? (You bet)
Are you a world traveler? (Wishing)
Do you like me? (Sometimes)
Are you lots of fun? (Never)
Do you love your husband? (I'm thinking)
Do you think you are sexy? (Absolutely)
Do you think that I might be good conversationalist? (You hope)
Can you tell me some of your love secrets? (Whatever)
Are you madly in love with someone? (Crazy About You)

We played this game and the guests enjoyed being participants.

The game for this party is a wedding word scramble.
The person that can figure out the most answers on this scramble wins the prize.

Wedding Word Scramble

1. oonmyhneo — — — — — — — — —

2. edbir — — — — —

3. rrmegaai — — — — — — — —

4. ormnaec — — — — — — —

5. fgti — — — —

6. velo — — — —

7. diam fo onhro — — — — — — — — — — —

8. wong — — — —

9. styhailer — — — — — — — — —

10. subhand — — — — — — —

11. ridmedbais — — — — — — — — — —

12. adddy's ttiell irgl — — — — — — — — — — — — — — — —

13. grthproophay — — — — — — — — — — —

14. ddwegni grni — — — — — — — — — — —

15. camphange — — — — — — — — —

16. cerpenoti — — — — — — — — —

17. feiw — — — —

18. eahrt — — — — —

19. ddewgin keca — — — — — — — — — —

20. etbs mna — — — — — — —

Wedding Word Scramble Key
The Color Chart Game

1.honeymoon 2. bride 3. marriage 4. romance 5.gift 6. Love 7. maid of honor 8. gown 9. hairstyle 10. husband 11. bridesmaid 12. Daddy's little girl 13.photography 14.wedding ring 15. champagne 16. reception 17.wife 18.heart 19. wedding cake 20. best man

Hand out each guest a color chart sheet. Using the color chart, find and circle the color which you think best describes you. Ask one of the guests to guess your color that best fits you.

▪	**Red**	**Love and Passion, Power and Strength, Courage and Respect**
▪	**Orange**	**Desire and Sensuality, Happiness and Bliss, Creativity and Enjoyment**
▪	**Blue**	**Tranquility and Peace, Coolness and Calm, Truth and Wisdom**
▪	**Green**	**Growth and Prosperity, Harmony and Balance, Hope and Luck**
▪	**Purple**	**Majesty and Dignity, Ambition and Success, Relaxation and Enchantment. Love at First Sight and Everlasting Love**
▫	**White**	**Elegance and Grace, Purity and Goodness, Loyalty and Devotion**
▪	**Yellow**	**Warmth and Healing, Confidence and Trust, Lightness and Gaiety**
▪	**Pink**	**Innocence and Femininity Friendship and Kindness, Peace and Joy**
▪	**Brown**	**Ease and Comfort Earthy and Natural**

A Casual Berry Beary Christmas Menu

Creamy Chicken Soup

Raspberry Salmon Lettuce Salad

Cranberry Muffins

Wheat Rolls

Butter

Beary Brownies

Coffee and Milk

A Casual Berry Beary Christmas Bridal Shower Theme

Tip

Brown rice can be found in the frozen food department. Purchase cooked wild rice in 15-ounce cans and frozen skinless, boneless chicken breasts in the freezer, deli or meat department at your local grocery store. Chicken breasts can also be purchased frozen in 6 pound bags. Just weigh out the amount of chicken breasts needed and place the pieces on a plate or microwave dish. Microwave for 5-10 minutes or until chicken is no longer pink. Cool and cube the chicken breasts. Add cubed chicken to the soup. The combination of the three soups listed below in the cream of mushroom and chicken soup recipe make the perfect base for this quick and easy soup.

Most people do not own a stockpot big enough to make 50 servings so use two stockpots and make 2 batches of 25 servings.

Creamy Chicken Soup
Yield: 12 servings

2-10¾ ounce cans (each) cream of mushroom soup
2-10¾ ounce cans (each) cream of chicken soup
1-10¾ ounce can cream of cheddar cheese soup
1-15 ounce can plus 1 cup chicken stock
1-12 ounce can evaporated milk
1 cup cooked wild rice (from a can)
1 cup cooked brown rice
1½ cups frozen peas, thawed
¾ cup shredded carrots
2 tablespoons minced onion
1½ teaspoons minced garlic
2 tablespoons dehydrated red bell pepper
3 tablespoons dehydrated celery flakes
1/3 cup warm water
½ teaspoon white pepper
1 teaspoon curry powder
1 pound cooked chicken breast

Creamy Chicken Soup
Yield: 25 servings

1-3 pound 2 ounce can of cream of mushroom soup
1-3 pound 2 ounce can cream of chicken soup
2-10¾ ounce cans (each) cheddar cheese soup
3-15 ounce cans (each) chicken stock
2-12 ounce cans (each) evaporated milk
1-15 ounce can cooked wild rice
2 cups cooked brown rice
3 cups frozen peas, thawed
1¼ cup shredded carrots
¼ cup minced onion
1 tablespoon minced garlic
¼ cup dehydrated red bell pepper
1/3 cup dehydrated celery flakes
1 cup warm water
1 teaspoon white pepper
2 teaspoons curry powder
2 pounds cooked chicken breast

Creamy Chicken Soup, continued

Place warm water in a small bowl. Add the dehydrated onion, red bell pepper and celery flakes. Let stand for 5 minutes to soften the vegetables. Drain the water off the vegetables. Set aside. Follow package directions and microwave the brown rice. In a large stockpot, place the cream of mushroom, cream of chicken and cheddar cheese soup. Stir in the chicken stock and evaporated milk. Add the wild and brown rice, peas, carrots, minced onion, minced garlic, dehydrated vegetables, white pepper, curry powder and cubed chicken. Thoroughly stir all ingredients until well blended. Simmer on low heat, stirring occasionally, for about ½ hour or until heated through. Serve soup in a large crock pot and serve with a basket of crackers.

Tip

One 16 ounce bottle of lemon pepper marinade will marinate 12 individual salmon portions. Twelve pieces of salmon should fit on an 11x17 broiler pan. The salmon filets should be skinless, boneless and approximately 1 inch thick.

Raspberry Salmon Lettuce Salad
Yield: 12 servings

1-48 ounce bag frozen skinless salmon fillets
1-16 ounce bottle lemon pepper marinade
Olive oil
1-46 ounce package spring lettuce
1 pound fresh strawberries, cleaned,
 hulled and sliced
1-6 ounce container fresh raspberries
1 pint blueberries
2-15 ounce cans (each) Mandarin
 oranges, drained and patted dry
1 cup whole pecans, divided
1 cup Craisins®, divided
3 lemons cut into wedges, divided
1-12 ounce bottle raspberry vinaigrette
12-8 inch doilies

Brush lemon pepper marinade on the top and bottom of each piece of salmon. Refrigerate for one hour. Place salmon pieces on the broiler pan. Brush the top

Raspberry Salmon Lettuce Salad, continued

with olive oil. Broil salmon on the top rack of oven for 6-8 minutes. Turn salmon over and brush the bottom with olive oil. Continue to broil for approximately 6-8 more minutes. Place individual servings on a tray and cool. Cover and refrigerate. Rinse off the lettuce, strawberries, raspberries, blueberries and Mandarin oranges. Dab dry. In a large bowl mix together the lettuce and the four varieties of fruits. Divide the salad among 12 salad bowls and place on plates lined with a doily. Place one piece of cooked salmon on top of each salad. Garnish each salad with pecans and Craisins®; serve two lemon wedges on each salad with raspberry vinaigrette dressing on the side. Refer to page 225 for recipe for multi grain rolls.

Tip

Each 19.95 ounce box of chewy fudge brownies makes 6 beary brownies. A special shaped pan contains 6 individual bears. Brownies can be made ahead of time and frozen without the powdered sugar. If you do not want to frost the brownies or cake decorate each bear, sprinkle with a light dusting of powdered sugar while bears are still warm. Brownies can be made three days in advance and do not need to be refrigerated. One suggestion is to make a batch of butter cream frosting and cake decorate each bear with a number 30 star tip. Another decorative alternative is to use creamy peanut butter in a pastry bag and a number 7 writing tip to pipe on paws, ears, eyes, mouth and nose.

Beary Brownies
Yield: 6 brownies

1-19.25 ounce box chewy
  fudge brownie mix
water
oil
no-stick baking spray
3 tablespoons powdered sugar, divided
1-12 inch red shaped heart doily

Beary Brownie Bears Decorated
with Peanut Butter

Use the suggested amounts of ingredients and follow the directions on the back of the brownie mix box. Spray no-stick baking spray in each individual bear mold. Evenly divide the batter among the six bears. Bake at 350F for 15-18 minutes. Cool brownies in the pan on a cooling rack for 15 minutes. Gently turn the pan upside down and remove the 6 bears. Sprinkle the bears with a light dusting of powdered sugar. Place bears on a platter lined with a heart doily. (See photo above).

Coffee and Milk Detail

See coffee and milk detail in the Fallen in Love chapter on page 188.

How to Set Up the Casual Berry Beary Christmas Buffet (from Left to Right)

Cover the buffet with a red tablecloth.

1. Alternate green and red napkins on the buffet.
2. Place soup spoons and soup bowls next to the napkins.
3. Place serving soup spoon on spoon rest between the soup bowls and crock pot.
4. Place soup into crock pot next to the soup bowls.
5. Place the salad forks in between the rolls and butter pats.

Brownie Setup with Bride and Groom Bears

6. Place a Christmas candle next to the cracker basket.
7. Place the salads next to the rolls. Place the Santa Claus salt and pepper shakers behind the salads.
8. Place the lemon wedges and the raspberry dressing behind the salads.
9. Place decorated brownies in front of the bride and groom bears.
10. At random, decorate the buffet table with clumps of berries.

Soup Setup

Rolls and Salads Setup

The Good Wishes Game

Using the beary brownies, place a long thin candle in each decorated bear. Light each candle and ask each guest to select a bear with lite candle and also make a wish for the happy couple.

Examples of Good Wishes

1. I wish you a long and happy life.
2. I wish that we will all remain good friends.
3. I wish you much success as a couple.
4. I wish that you will always love each other.
5. I wish much success in your marriage as a team.
6. I wish you many blessings throughout the years.

Brownie Bears of Good Wishes

7. I wish you many joys and beautiful experiences as a couple.
8. I wish you many happy memories as a couple.
9. I wish you will always laugh and enjoy life together.
10. I wish you great growth of your love for each other in years ahead.

Now you can add your own wishes and even add funny wedding wishes.

Salmon Salads and Brownie Dessert Platters with Bride and Groom Bears

The Engagement
Announcement
Social by Mrs. T's Menu

Apple Coffee Cake
Cranberry Coffee Cake
Flying Flamingo Pineapple
Cheese and Meat Tree
Deviled Eggs
A Mirror Tray with Magic Bars,
Pecan Fingers and Russian Tea Cakes
Sweet Rolls
Tuna Fish Dip
Cheese Board Tray
Assorted Crackers
Chicken Roll-Ups
Festive Tropical Fruit Salad
Christmas Wreath Fudge
Holiday Punch
Coffee, Cream, Sugar

Chapter 10
The Engagement Announcement Social by Mrs. T
Mrs. T's Bridge Club Party

Mrs. T's Story

Mrs. T worked out religiously at the YMCA. She was petite and very fit. She groomed herself daily in the lady's locker room after exercising. She listened to everyone talk about their children getting married, and also becoming a grandmother. She always listened and congratulated each YMCA member. However, deep down she felt the pain of the lack of her daughter's wedding bells and becoming a grandmother. She lost her son in the war and worked hard to accept his death. Her daughter, Christine was a beautiful young lady. She was smart, witty, kind and just a perfect daughter. Deep down, her heart ached that her daughter just could not find Mr. Right. In fact her daughter didn't even seem interested in dating. She was very career minded and loved her job.

Her daughter Christine also felt the pain of losing her brother Bill in the war. She wanted to join the army about the time her brother joined. Her mother said no. She wanted to tell her mom that she really needed to join the army. About six months after her brother's death, Christine finally approached her mom and announced that she was going to join the service. Her mother knew that she had to let go and became supportive of her daughter's decision. Christine was happy that her mom would let her join.

Christine made a career of the army for the next 14 years. Time was ticking away. How did those years fly by so quickly? Christine just turned 34. Mrs. T was concerned that Christine would be alone if something happened her.

Christine called her mom on Thanksgiving Day. She asked her mom to talk with her via satellite. To her mother's surprise she introduced her to Dean, her fiancé. Both were very excited and told Mrs. T that they were happy. Mrs. T thought that Dean was very personable.

Cranberry Coffee Cake

Yield: One Bundt pan
(16 servings)

1-8 ounce package Neufchatel
  cheese, softened
1 cup butter, softened
1¼ cups sugar
1 teaspoon orange flavoring
1 teaspoon orange peel
4 eggs
2¼ cups flour, divided
1½ teaspoons baking powder
1 teaspoon cinnamon
2½ cups fresh cranberries
½ cup pecans, finely chopped
no-stick baking spray
1-12 inch doily

Glaze Topping

½ cup powdered sugar
3 tablespoons water
1 teaspoon orange flavoring
¼ teaspoon salt
½ cup pecans, chopped
⅓ cup Craisins®, optional

Cranberry Coffee Cake

Beat together Neufchatel cheese and butter until creamy. Add the sugar and beat. Add the orange flavoring, orange peel and eggs. Beat. Stir 1 cup of flour into the cranberries. Set aside. Add 1¼ cups flour, baking powder and cinnamon to the butter mixture. Stir in the cranberries and pecans. Place batter into a greased Bundt pan with no-stick baking spray. Bake at 350F for 55-60 minutes or until toothpick inserted in the center comes out clean. Cool for 5 minutes. Stir water, orange flavoring and salt into the powdered sugar until smooth. Set aside. Place the doily on a footed 12-inch tray and turn the coffee cake onto the serving tray. Gently spoon the glaze topping mixture over the top of the coffee cake. Sprinkle pecans and Craisins® on the top of the coffee cake. On the day of the party cut the coffee cake into 16 servings. (See photo above).

Flying Flamingo Pineapple Cheese and Meat Tree
Yield: 20 servings

For details on how to make the pineapple tree refer to page 50 in Chapter 3. Instead of using all cheese, use a one pound package of slim jim sticks, cut the slim jim sticks into 6 pieces. Alternate the cheese with the meat in the middle and cheese on the top and bottom of cheese of the Flamingo stir stick. (See photo on page 240).

Deviled Eggs
Yield: 24 deviled eggs

12 hard cooked eggs
3 teaspoons lemon juice, divided
1¼ teaspoons salt, divided
¼ teaspoon pepper
½ cup mayonnaise
2 teaspoons sugar
2 teaspoons yellow mustard
¼ teaspoon Worcestershire sauce

Deviled Eggs
Yield: 50 deviled eggs

25 hard cooked eggs
5 teaspoons lemon juice, divided
2½ teaspoons salt, divided
½ teaspoon pepper
1¼ cup mayonnaise
1 tablespoon sugar
1 teaspoon yellow mustard
½ teaspoon Worcestershire sauce

Add eggs to an appropriate size pan with cold water. Add ¾ teaspoon salt and 1½ teaspoons lemon juice for the 24 yield size batch of eggs. Add 1¼ teaspoon salt and 2½ teaspoons lemon juice for the 50 yield size batch of eggs. Bring to a boil and boil for 5- 8 minutes. Shut off the eggs. Remove eggs from the stove. Cover the eggs for 30 minutes and let the eggs finish cooking. Run cold water over the eggs. When eggs are cool enough to handle, peel them and cut in half lengthwise. Scoop out the yolks and place into a mixing bowl. Carefully set the egg whites aside. Beat egg yolks until they are fine particles. Add mayonnaise and beat until smooth. Add remaining lemon juice, salt, pepper, sugar, mustard and Worcestershire sauce. Beat until smooth and creamy. Insert a 1E cake tube into a 12 inch pastry bag. Fill the pastry bag three-quarters full. Fill each reserved egg white half. Garnish with paprika and parsley.

Magic Bars
Yield: 16 bars

Crust
½ cup butter
1 cup graham cracker crumbs

Magic Bars, continued

Topping

1 cup coconut
1 cup pecans, chopped
1 cup semisweet mini
  chocolate chips
1 cup Christmas M&M's
1-14 ounce can sweetened condensed milk

Preheat oven to 350F. Melt butter in microwave and pour into a 9x9x2 inch pan. Spread graham cracker crumbs evenly over the melted butter to form a crust. Top with coconut. Top with nuts. Sprinkle chocolate chips over nuts. Pour sweetened condensed milk evenly over the top of the chocolate chips. Sprinkle Christmas M&M's on top. Bake for 25-30 minutes or until golden brown. Cool slightly. Cut into bars. (See chart on page 106 for cutting bars).

Pecan Fingers and Russian Tea Cakes
Yield: 30 pecan fingers
Yield: 30 Russian tea cakes

2 cups butter
1 cup powdered sugar
2 teaspoons vanilla
4½ cups flour
½ teaspoon salt
¾ cup walnuts, finely chopped
¾ cup pecans, finely chopped
20 miniature candy canes

Magic Bars, Pecan Fingers and Russian Tea Cakes

Mix butter, sugar and vanilla thoroughly. Stir in flour and salt. Divide the dough in half and place into two separate bowls (approximately 1½ pounds per bowl). Add the walnuts to one bowl and the pecans to the other bowl. Mix nuts into doughs. Roll the dough with walnuts into 1 inch balls and form finger shapes with the pecan dough. Place cookies on an ungreased baking sheet (cookies do not spread). Bake at 400F for 10 to 12 minutes or until set. Cookies should not be brown on top, but slightly browned on the bottom of each cookie. Roll each cookie into powdered sugar. Cool. Arrange on mirror serving tray with magic bars. Decorate with candy canes. (See photo above).

Orange Danish
Yield: 10 orange Danish
sweet rolls

2-17.5 ounce cans (each)
  jumbo orange Danish
  with icing (5 per can)

Place Danish on baking sheet. Follow directions on the can. Frost Danish with icing after baked while Danish is still warm. Cool. Place on tiered tray. Serve.

Cinnamon Rolls
Yield: 16 cinnamon rolls

2-13 ounce cans (each)
  flaky cinnamon rolls with
  icing (8 per can)
Place cinnamon rolls on baking sheet. Follow directions on the can. Frost with icing after cinnamon rolls are baked. Cool. Place on tiered tray with the Danish.

Tuna Fish Dip
Yield: 20 servings

2-8 ounce packages (each)
 cream cheese, softened
2-6 ounce packages (each) tuna
1/3 cup celery, diced
2 teaspoons dehydrated
  minced onions
1 teaspoon minced garlic
1 teaspoon Worcestershire sauce
2 teaspoons curry powder
½ teaspoon salt
½ teaspoon pepper
1 black olive
1 cup slivered almonds
1 bunch parsley
paprika
1 pound Ritz® crackers

Tuna Fish Dip

In a five quart mixing bowl, beat cream cheese. Drain and dry tuna. Add the tuna, celery, onions, garlic, Worcestershire sauce, curry powder, salt and pepper to the cream cheese. Beat until smooth and creamy. Shape dip into a fish. Lightly sprinkle paprika over the entire body of the fish dip. Place black olive in the head area to form an eye. Place slivered almonds in rows over the entire body of the fish to form scales. Garnish with parsley. Serve with Ritz® crackers or crackers of choice. (See photo on page 233).

Cheese Tray Board

Cheese Tray Board with Cheese Ball

Bacon Cheese Ball
Yield: 25
1-12 ounce container bacon
 cheese spread, softened
1-8 ounce package
 cream cheese, softened
1 teaspoon Worcestershire sauce
1 teaspoon dehydrated
 minced onions
1 cup walnuts, finely chopped

Beat together the bacon cheese spread and cream cheese until smooth and creamy. Add the Worcestershire sauce and the minced onions. Beat. Shape mixture into a ball. Roll into the chopped walnuts. Refrigerate for an hour.

Cheese Slices
Yield: 25 servings

1 pound havarti cheese
½ pound aged cheddar cheese
½ pound feta cheese
½ pound red grapes
1 bunch parsley

Place the cheese ball in the center of the cheese tray board. Slice and cut the havarti, cheddar and feta cheese into squares to fit each cracker. Starting right to left and left to right, place one row havarti, cheddar and feta cheese toward the cheese ball. Place a row of havarti around the cheese ball to form a horseshoe effect. Garnish cheese ball with grapes and parsley. Serve with snowman cheese spreader knife. (See photo on page 241).

Crackers
Yield: 25 servings
1 pound of party crackers
  of choice

Line a basket with a napkin. Place crackers into the lined basket and serve with the cheese and fish dip

Chicken Roll-Ups
Yield: 40 rolls ups

2-13 ounce cans (each)
  premium chunk chicken
1/3 cup shredded carrots
1/3 cup celery, diced
1/3 cup red onion, diced
1/3 cup yellow bell pepper, diced
1 tablespoon minced garlic
1 tablespoon dehydrated chives
1 cup Mexican blend cheese
½ teaspoon salt
1 teaspoon white pepper
1 teaspoon cumin
1 cup mayonnaise
10-6 inch soft flour tortillas
½ cup butter, softened
1-12 inch doily

Chicken Roll-Ups

Drain and dry the chicken. Add the carrots, celery, onion, bell pepper, garlic, chives, cheese, salt, pepper and cumin. Moisten ingredients with the mayonnaise. On the day of the party, lay out 10 tortillas. Lightly spread butter over each tortilla. Divide the chicken filling among the 10 tortillas (about 1/3 cup per tortilla). Spread filling over each shell. Roll up and cut each roll up into 4 pieces. Arrange on a 12 inch tray lined with a doily and also with a candle in the center of the tray. (See photo above).

Festive Tropical Fruit Salad
Yield: 20 servings

2 granny smith apples,
  with peelings, cored and
  chopped
2 gala apples, with
  peelings, cored and
  chopped
1-16 ounce can pineapple
  chunks, drained
1-11 ounce can Mandarin
  oranges
1-15 ounce can tropical
  fruit, drained
½ pound whole red grapes, cleaned
⅓ cup celery, finely
  chopped
1 pomegranate
1-16 ounce container
  light sour cream
1-8 ounce package
  Neufchatel cheese, softened
1 tablespoon Splenda®
3 tablespoons amaretto liqueur
1 teaspoon cinnamon
2 drops red food coloring
1 head red kale
1 bunch parsley

Festive Tropical Fruit Salad

Place chopped apples in a large bowl. Add the pineapple, Mandarin oranges, tropical fruit, grapes and celery. Set aside. Peel the pomegranate and remove seeds. Set aside. In a five quart mixer, mix together the sour cream, Neufchatel cheese, Splenda®, amaretto liqueur, cinnamon and food coloring. Stir fruit into Neufchatel cream cheese mixture. Clean and dry the kale leaves and parsley. Place the fruit salad into a large pasta bowl. Place kale around the outer edge of the salad. Garnish with pomegranate seeds and parsley. (See photo above).

Christmas Wreath Fudge

Yield: 20-24 servings

1-10 ounce package Andres® crème de menthe baking chips
1-12 ounce package mini semi sweet chocolate chips
¾ cup pecans, finely chopped
1-14 ounce can sweetened condensed milk
1 empty condensed milk can
16 miniature size candy canes, divided
6 green maraschino cherries

Christmas Wreath Fudge

In top of a double boiler, add the crème de menthe baking chips, chocolate chips, pecans and sweetened condensed milk. Stir ingredients together until chocolate is melted and fudge is smooth. Remove from the stove and cool for 5 minutes. Place sweetened condensed milk can in a center of a 12 inch glass tray. Place fudge around the can to form a wreath. Place 6 miniature candy canes in a bag. Close bag. With a rolling pin crush the candy canes into tiny pieces. Sprinkle the crushed candy canes over the top of the fudge. Place 10 candy canes around the outer edge of the fudge. Evenly distribute the 6 maraschino cherries on the top of the fudge in a circle-like fashion. Remove the can from the center of the fudge. Cut fudge into 20-24 wedges before serving time. (See photo above).

Holiday Punch
Yield: 25 servings

1 liter bottle 7-UP®, divided
1 quart pineapple juice
1 gallon berry rush punch
1 star ice mold
1 orange

Pour half of the 7-UP® into the star ice mold. Freeze for 24 hours. On the day of the party add the remaining half of 7-UP®, half of the pineapple juice and half of the berry rush punch into a large punch bowl. Unmold the ice mold. Place into the punch. Slice orange into 6 slices and garnish the top of the punch with orange slices. Serve in holiday throw away cups. (See photo on page 240).

Coffee Detail
Yield: 32 cups decaf coffee

1¾ cups decaf coffee
32 cups water
1 pint cream
1 cup sugar
1 bowl with sugar substitute

Using a large percolator pot, fill with water up to the 32 cup line. Place the stem into the hole of the coffee pot. Slide basket into the stem. Place coffee into the basket. Cover basket with the lid. Perk coffee 35-40 minutes before guests arrive.

Coffee Detail
Yield: 12 cups regular coffee

12 cups water
1 coffee filter
¾ cup regular coffee

Fill coffee pot to the 12 cup line. Place coffee filter into the basket. Place coffee into filter. Perk 10-15 minutes before guests arrive. Serve in holiday throw away cups.

Reindeer Memories Step by Step Illustrations (fig. 1-6)
Yield: 1 Reindeer

2-8½x11 sheet (brown
 construction paper)
1 pencil
1 pair paper scissors
1 bottle all purpose glue
1 red pom-pom
1 dime

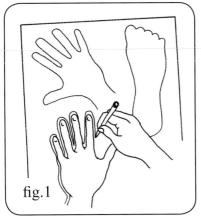

fig.1

Trace the right and left hand and right foot.

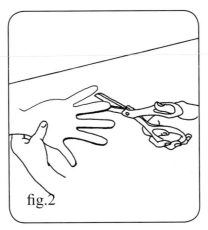

fig.2

Cut out the hands and foot.

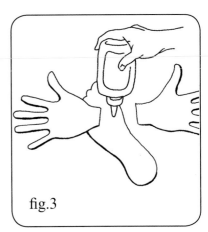

fig.3

Glue hands on top of the back side of the foot.

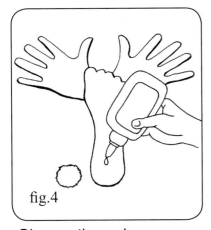

fig.4

Glue on the red pom-pom.

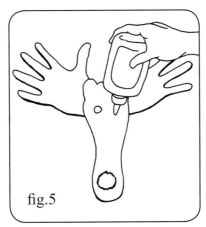

fig.5

Using a dime, trace and cut out the eyes and glue them onto the reindeer.

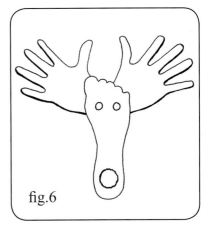

fig.6

See finish project.

Now all the guests are ready to write a beautiful wedding wish to Christine.

Guest Tables Setup

Set up two guest tables (8 per table). Cover each table with a holiday tablecloth. Place a small centerpiece of choice in the center of the table for decoration. Do not set the table. Let the people sit wherever they want to sit. The conversation is very interesting and fun.

The Engagement Announcement Social Buffet Setup

For this casual gathering, cover the center of the buffet area with 10 Christmas design placemats in a row. Follow the photos and steps to lay out the buffet starting left to right. See photos on page photos below.

1. Holiday cups for punch
2. Holiday cocktail napkins
3. Holiday 7 inch plates
4. Plain white 10 inch plates
5. In back of the plates is a snowman.
6. In a footed glass lying on its side are forks.
7. To the right of the white divided plates is a tiered tray with apple coffee cake.
8. To the right of the apple coffee cake is a footed cake serving plate with the cranberry coffee cake decorated with a poinsettia silk flower in the center.
9. Behind the cranberry coffee, is the flying flamingo pineapple cheese and meat tree.
10. To the right of the flying flamingo pineapple cheese and meat tree are the deviled eggs in Mrs. T's favorite chicken baskets.

Coffee Cake and Flying
Flamingo Pineapple Cheese
and Meat Tree Setup

Punch and Coffee Cake Setup

Cookie Tray and Deviled Eggs Setup

11. The mirror holding the magic bars, pecan fingers and Russian tea cakes is in front of the chicken baskets with deviled eggs. The center of the mirror is decorated with poinsettia silk flowers. Each end of the mirror is decorated with miniature candy canes.
12. Next to the deviled eggs are the sweet rolls.
13. In front of the sweet rolls is the tuna dip.
14. Next to the sweet rolls and tuna dip is a small decorated Christmas tree.
15. In front of the tree is a pair of salt and pepper shakers.
16. To the right of the Christmas tree are 3 poinsettia centerpieces.
17. In front of the salt and pepper shakers is the cheese board tray.
18. Behind the cheese board tray is a basket of assorted crackers.
19. Behind the crackers is a pepper mill.
20. Next to the pepper mill are 3 more poinsettia centerpieces.
21. To the right of the basket of crackers is a tray of chicken roll-ups with a snowman candle centerpiece.
22. To the right of the chicken roll-ups is the festive fruit salad.
23. To the right of the festive fruit salad is the fudge garnished with candy canes.
24. To the right of the fudge is the crib scene
25. To the right of the crib scene is an angel.

Cheese Board with Crackers and Chicken Roll-Ups

Tuna Fish Dip and Sweet Rolls

Crib Scene

Chicken Roll-Ups and Festive Salad

Mrs. T's
Bridge Club
Party Menu

Chicken Spaghetti Bake
Green Salad
Italian Dressing
Fresh Fruit Plate
Garlic Crescent Rolls
Chocolate Caramel Bars
Grandma's Cranberry
Surprise Pie

Mrs. T's Bridge Club Party

In the evening, Mrs. T played bridge with her friends. They decided to bring their favorite recipes and also bring a dish to pass for the entire meal. They wanted to celebrate with Mrs. T upon learning about her daughter's engagement. Mrs. T was delighted with the meal and she would make sure that her daughter and future son-in-law would receive the recipes.

Mrs. Martin showed off her chicken spaghetti bake. Emily made a wonderful green salad with Italian dressing. Mrs. T's mom Hazel made a simple fruit plate. Clare made her favorite chocolate caramel bars and garlic rolls. Bee made her grandma's surprised pie recipe. Have fun making these recipes too!

Chicken Spaghetti Bake
Yield: 8-10 servings

12-ounces wheat spaghetti (¾ of a 1 pound box)
2 tablespoons olive oil
water
salt
4-8 ounce boneless skinless
  chicken breasts (each), cubed
1 cup chicken broth
½ cup red onion, diced
1 cup fresh mushrooms, chopped
½ yellow bell pepper, diced
½ green bell pepper, diced
1 tablespoon minced garlic
2-10 ounce cans (each)
  diced tomatoes and green chilies
1-24 ounce Bertolli®
  organic olive oil, basil and garlic
  spaghetti sauce
1-6 ounce can tomato paste
1 teaspoon Italian seasoning
½ teaspoon salt
1 teaspoon white pepper
2 cups shredded mozzarella cheese
olive oil-cooking spray

Chocolate Caramel Bars, continued

and sprinkle with the chocolate chips and walnuts. In a small bowl, combine caramel topping with ⅓ cup flour. Drizzle over the chocolate chips and walnuts. Sprinkle with the remaining crumb mixture. Bake at 350F for 20-25 minutes more or until browned. Cool. Cut into 30 bars.

Bridge Club Wishes

At the bridge club dinner, the ladies showed excitement for Mrs. T's daughter's engagement. They wanted to make all kinds of suggestions and also help. Mrs. T said, "Wait! I don't want to interfere with my daughter's ideas for planning her wedding. Whatever she wants is just fine with me. My mother let me know that she was in charge of my wedding day plans. Needless to say, there was great tension between us and also the rest of our family. It really put a damper on my wedding. I do not want to repeat that for my daughter. A wedding day is supposed to be filled with love and happiness. I want to make sure that my daughter has a wonderful day and a great beginning to a happy marriage. I want to thank all of you for your kind offer. Please just be there for my daughter and enjoy the day". Her bridge club friends agreed to be there and also be supportive of Christine's wishes.

Bee's Cranberry Surprise Pie and Story About Her Grandmother

Bee came late and brought a cranberry surprise pie for dessert and the recipe for Christine. She told her story to her bridge friends, "I was thinking about my grandmother today. She was born in Belgium and she came across the ocean when she was only 16 years old. She loved to bake. She made the best pies. She always used lard when making her pie crusts. Every Thanksgiving she made a pie without a bottom crust. She called it a cranberry surprise pie. She never gave me the recipe no matter how many times I asked her. After her death I found this recipe but it was written in her own native language. My aunt helped me translate the recipe. My aunt told me that she never measured anything. It was a pinch of this or that".

Bee stated that with practice she mastered her grandmother's cranberry surprise pie. Bee wanted to share the pie and also the recipe with her bridge friends.

Grandma's Surprise Pie
Yield: 1-9 inch pie

¼ cup butter, melted
2 granny smith apples
1½ cups fresh cranberries

⅓ cup sugar
¼ teaspoon cinnamon
⅓ cup sliced almond nuts
  or chopped pecans

My Crust Topping
Yield: 1-9 inch pie crust topping

½ cup butter, softened
½ cup brown sugar
1 cup flour
1 tablespoon cinnamon-sugar

Melt butter in microwave. Pour ¼ cup melted butter into the 9 inch pie pan and coat the bottom and sides of the pan. Peel, core, and thinly slice the apples. Cut cranberries in half. Place apples and cranberries into buttered pie pan. Mix together the ⅓ cup sugar with ¼ teaspoon cinnamon. Sprinkle sugar mixture over the fruit and toss together. Sprinkle the almond nuts or pecans over the fruit. Set aside. Beat together butter and the brown sugar until smooth and creamy. Add the flour and beat until blended together to make a crumbly topping. Sprinkle the topping over the entire top of the pie to form the crust and also sealing the crust with the crust topping. Bake at 350F for 35-45 minutes or until apples are soft and the crust is golden brown.

Grandma's Crust Topping
Yield: l-9 inch pie crust topping

2 tablespoons butter, melted
⅔ cup flour
1 egg
½ cup sugar
1 tablespoon cinnamon-sugar

Add the butter to the flour, egg and sugar. Beat until smooth. Sprinkle the cinnamon-sugar over the pie crust topping. Bake at 350F for 35-45 minutes or until apples are soft and crust is golden brown.

Everyone enjoyed Bee's Grandma's surprise pie recipe. The evening was successful, creating new excitement for Christine's upcoming wedding.

Index

Chicken Recipes:

Chocolate Recipes:

Coffee Cake Recipes:

Coffee Detail:

Color:

Cookies:

Crab:

Crêpes:

D
Decorations

Diagrams and Steps:

Meats:

Menus for Each Chapter:

N
Napkin Detail:

O
Orange:

Parties:

Photos and Illustrations:

Y

Yeast Breads:

Z